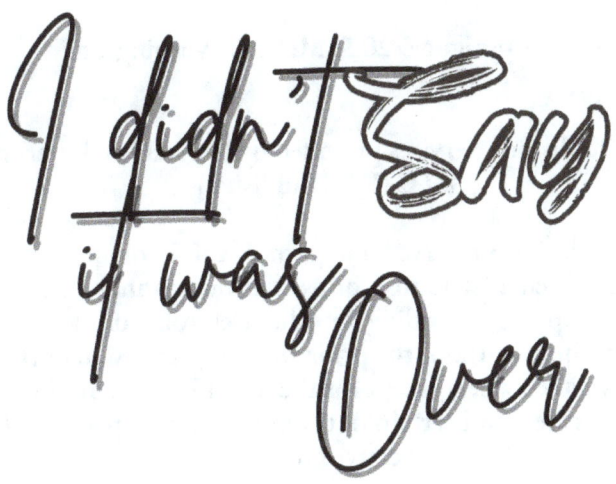

by
Melvina W

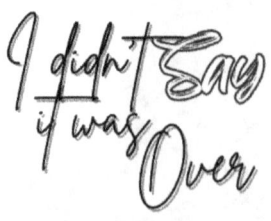

Copyright © 2024 Melvina Washington

Self Publishing Services provided by Krystal Lee Enterprises LLC (KLE Publishing)

All rights reserved. No parts of this book may be reproduced, distributed, or used in any manner, including photocopying, recording, or other electronic or mechanical methods without the prior written permission of the copywriter owner, except for the use of brief quotations in a book review and certain noncommercial uses permitted by copyright law.

Paperback: 978-1-945066-64-1

Please send comments and questions for Publishing to:
Krystal Lee Enterprises
sales@KLEPub.com

To Reach the Author:
Email: info@IAmMelvina.com

Web: IAMMelvina.com
Contact: Phone: 815-635-8462
Printed in the United States of America.

Disclaimers
The information in this book was correct at the time of publication, but the Author does not assume any liability for loss or damage caused by errors or omissions. These are my memories, from my perspective, and I have tried to represent events as faithfully as possible.

Dedication

For my lover, my best friend, the only man of my life, my husband Glenn

For my three grown daughters, who I love unconditionally and forever will until I die, Mariama, Sierra, and Amira

For my parents who taught me love, gave me love, and I have loved since the beginning of time, Melvin and Albertha

And to any person that believes in yourself, dreams big, works hard, plays harder, and TRULY believes in infinite possibilities that "I Did Not Say It Was Over." You still need to make things happen "Come Hell or High Water" …

And, in the near future I wil tell you that some things you will have to "Let It Go!"

-This book is for YOU!

Table of Contents

Introduction: I AM Melvina	7
Chapter One: In the Beginning	13
Chapter Two: Finding Love	31
Chapter Three: When Life Heats UP	43
Chapter Four: Motivation	63
Chapter Five: What it Takes	73
Chapter Six: Solid Foundation	85
Chapter Seven: Dream Big!	95
Chapter Eight: Starting on the Path	103
Chapter Nine: Overcoming Challenges	113
Chapter Ten: Resources	123
Chapter Eleven: About Melvina Washington	129

Introduction

I Didn't Say it Was Over!

There is levels to this.

We often say that when I arrive and start making money, life will get easier. The truth is, it doesn't. You do get a lot more options. For me, making money is what I do–and I love to make it. Not because I am a heartless, money-hungry woman but because I enjoy what money can provide: options.

When I was growing up (if you read book one, **Come Hell or High Water**), you would know I grew up with no silver spoon in my mouth. My parents were loving and kind to me, but they had a different thought process than mine. My dad and I are the most alike, but he made different choices and always told me to do better than Mom and him.

My mother was loving and kind. She wanted me to follow the traditional role of a wife, and I was grateful for what she taught me. But I still needed to become Melvina and not just Marie. We all have childhood names that we grow fond of. People see you as one thing, and it is hard for some people to see you blossom right before their eyes.

Some people want you to become what you need to be for them, while others want to use you–and not always in a bad way. In the background, you have music playing to accomplish your personal goals. How do you balance making others happy and yourself? Accomplishing your goals and elevating your career–even when challenges come your way?

You have to determine firstly to make it–Come Hell or High Water–but what do you do after that? What happens when you are married, you have the children you prayed for, and your job or career is moving in the right direction? You have to fight to maintain your growth and elevate from where you are now!

If you are ready to grow, I want you to journey with me through book two, "*I Didn't Say It Was Over*!"

Melvina W.

Catching You Up to Date!

Your crash course to Melvina--yes, deeper things than the first book.

In my first book, I know you might think I come off a bit strong. The truth is it has taken much time for me to muster the courage to hone my voice. Growing up in the South, dark skin, half deaf, heavy-set, loud, and different personality-wise weren't easy. It wasn't just people of other ethnicities who judged me for my appearance, but other black children, too. I had to learn some very hard lessons when I was young, which helped to prepare me for the woman I am today and shaped the mother I had to be for my daughters.

Let me explain. I was born with a nerve loss that rendered me 50% deaf at birth. My family was happy to oblige that adjustment, but children were another story. At home, my parents spoke at a level where I could hear them. I learned naturally to speak loud because I couldn't hear if I didn't do that.

I got hearing aids when I was young, and I used

them all throughout school. I remember when I started attending school. Many children appeared to have never seen a person using a hearing aid before. They would ask me several questions because they were curious and wanted to poke fun at me.

Hundreds of times, children would mouth words to me and motion their fingers to signal fake sign language at me. I could hear and see them, and honestly, their words hurt me so badly. I would go home and tell my parents about my day in tears. I can say that if my parents were not adamant about raising me to value myself, I would have had low self-esteem from school. Thank God that they always encouraged me.

When I wasn't being made fun of because of my hearing, I was called names because of my dark skin. I was told daily, "black is beautiful" by my mom, so I never thought about my complexion as anything out of the norm. School pumped the brakes on my utopia that race and colorism didn't exist amongst black people.

I was called every name under the sun, and black this or black that. Every day the children made it their business to point out how black I was, even giving me the name "Blackie." I didn't hate myself because my parents didn't allow me to act on that negativity.

I naturally gravitated to liking light-complexioned men because I never wanted my children to have to be teased like me. Two dark-complexioned people getting married and having children would result in dark-complexioned children unless somebody is lying

Melvina W.

Mr. and Mrs. Washington (Parents)

We knew since Marie was a little girl she would be great. She was born with a challenge and she cried about it a lot early on.

I never worried about her because I knew, the Father would not put on her more than she could handle.

Today, she is successful and she is doing us proud. We love her and are grateful for both of our loving children.

or smoking crack to believe otherwise. I am joking. I know there are real-life examples of that not being the case, but for me, it would definitely be the case.

If that wasn't enough, I had one more strike against me. I was always a big girl, ever since I could remember. Growing up, my parents were not concerned with the nutritional facts of food but with ensuring we didn't go to bed hungry. Feeding children with limited funds meant buying what you could afford and cooking how you knew how to make ends meet.

I was raised on a Southern diet–and no, it wasn't healthy, but it was what we knew. My mom cooked with lard, fried food, grease, and bacon, which, to me, made everything taste better. Soul food is still my preference, and I haven't been able to change that over the years. Back then, we didn't eat many fresh fruits and vegetables; they were more expensive than rice, beans, and other items. Most fresh veggies we got were boiled and piled in fat, and any nutritional value they had was likely reduced to none or very little.

I am still working on balancing my weight and having healthy boundaries with food–I didn't say it was over! I am in a growth process, too. I ain't never scared to admit that. The first step I had to learn to begin finding myself and really making a difference in my life was to be honest with Marie. I couldn't look at how many parents lived and make that my future.

I had to sit down and get to know what I wanted for life, and that didn't take me long. By the time I was thirteen, I knew I wanted a driver, a person to do my

Melvina W.

lawn care and to live in a large house. My education was going to pay for it. My dad harped on education and being better than him.

I knew being better off than my dad meant working smarter and just as hard. My dad was always a hard worker, and there wasn't anything he wouldn't do to help take care of our family. My mother taught me to have a loving heart and created a desire for a family. I grew up in a nuclear family with two parents who shared the same children (my brother and me).

This four-member family set the expectation for what I would like to have as a family unit and would also teach my daughters. I wanted my life to be similar to my parents', although I knew where I saw a divide. I didn't want to give away all that I had and end up with nothing. I enjoy giving back, but I had to have something to give. I desired more than what my parents had, and as I grew older–and even now, I want more!

I don't see myself stopping in my endeavor to make money, spend more time with my family, and be happy. For me, the three elements that are my cornerstones for life are family, love, and money. There is always room for the three to increase, so I will always be busy and want more of them. If you haven't considered your three elements (or how many you have) that drive you to work hard, take the time and jot them down now.

You will see that life gets a lot easier when what you are working so hard for is in view. I'm not saying life is peaches and cream; it's not, and challenges have been brewing in all three of my motivators at various

Catching You Up to Date

Terry Washington

I cannot write this book and not mention my brother whom I love dearly. I Did Not Say it Was Over!

When we lose people in our loves it can hurt us deeply and we may question what life will be like moving forward. I can tell you that it is not easy.

I miss him every day. He reminds me to live, love, and make sure I stay connected to family always.

Hugs and Love, Baby Brother

times in my life. But those challenges don't make me regret my progress and still push me along.

When life is getting tough for you, don't quit. Look back on what you have survived and see how you were strong enough to pivot, and then keep on pressing. I remember balling up in a corner and crying at school because the children were calling me a black pig, black cookie, and asking me demeaning questions like "What's wrong with you?", "Why you so black?", "What is that thing in your ear?"

I was an outcast growing up and thank God for the handful of good friends I acquired in school. Those friends encamped around me and would defend me. It is such a trigger for me to see children being bullied or having to watch ignorant people in 2024 do fake sign language to insult those short of hearing. I vowed then to make something of myself.

My mom always took the approach to ignore the people who talked about me. My dad didn't take that approach at all. He told me straight, "Marie, be better than all of them." I learned that money was an equalizer. The dark, light, skinny, or plumped could obtain it. Whoever got it, got the same respect because money has no name and doesn't care about what I look like.

Progress became my best friend. I wanted to be something that would make me proud of myself and know that I was somebody. I set my sights on education and always said I wouldn't be satisfied until I got at least a bachelors. I was so adamant about my standards that I didn't even walk and celebrate my associates. Not

Catching You Up to Date

because I wasn't proud I didn't want to be content with having less than I envisioned.

You best believe I went all out (celebratory-wise) when my bachelor's graduation day came. You have to determine not to settle for less than you want. What do you want and must have to feel like you?

I had to shift away from what made me feel inferior to what made me feel powerful. When I was made fun of because of my complexion, I watched and saw how other girls lighter than me were treated. Subconsciously, I thought being lighter meant being prettier for a long time.

It took most of my school years to get past it–if I can say I have. To be honest, some of our experiences can unintentionally stay with us all of our lives. I can still see the beauty in light complexion women, but a big difference: I can see the beauty in me. I can see beauty in me being fat, dark, loud, and half-deaf. This is what makes me content with my appearance, and perhaps that blocks me from losing weight.

Melvina W.

My husband loves me at this size, and I like weight on my bones. I ain't going to be a pencil. I know health is important, so I am doing Juice+, and I am a proud seller of it, too. If you want to get healthy and eat the fruits and vegetables you need daily in a gummy or tablet, scan the QR code, and let's get healthy together.

Some of us are beaten down and discouraged. Life feels like it isn't working. I want to tell you I found medical coding at a time when I needed it most! This field has helped me turn a lot of things around in my life. It is humbling to see the people today who made fun of me. They are not laughing at me anymore; we can laugh together as adults–and they respect me now.

I know it isn't all about the money. I am sure they had some personal growth as well. What I learned is that not everyone can see you the way you see yourself. Keep in mind that in Come Hell or High Water, my first book, I stated how I sat at the table at about nine or ten years old and claimed what I wanted. I said I wanted a maid; currently, I employ one. I am built differently. I was different then…and I still am different today.

Now, today, my difference is helping medical coders get jobs and muscle up the right attitude and mindset to come into this field and make good money. I am talking six figures for those who are motivated and have dreams to accomplish. I am not saying it is easy, it is work. But I am proof that the work can be done, and if you have me in your corner, I can make a world of difference.

Catching You Up to Date

When I was young, I couldn't keep coming to my parents crying about my problems. I had to find a solution. I needed to learn how to grow through my problems. If you are tired of bills, problems, and discouragement and want to change your life, Keep reading!

I was young and in school. I had a job, which was paying me well. I was a good talker and no pushover. I made my money as a server, and I was good at upselling. I bought my first house in my early twenties and never looked back. But soon after meeting the love of my life, Glenn, we were pregnant, married, and broke!

Having our first child added pressure, but the love we had kept us together. We were committed from the start, and we are still in love. I will tell you more about my boo in Chapter Three; just hold tight.

If you read my first book, I displayed pictures that show the naked truth about our love, commitment, and how we get down! Don't worry; the pictures are artistic and nothing pornographic–we have class! I hired a photographer and everything to help us celebrate my fiftieth birthday in Africa.

Something wonderful happens as we get older. We start to care less and less about what other people are saying. I have been clear on what I wanted most of my life, but at fifty, it went up a notch! Glenn and I are enjoying this empty nest phase if you catch my drift.

Back to my point, we had one daughter, and a

few years later, we added a pair of twins! Yes, we were running and robbing Peter to pay Paul. We were a work in progress, and we had to work together. I will always say I have a wonderful partner who has helped me become the owner, medical coder, and person I am today. I owe so much to Glenn.

Having three girls and a husband was work and sacrifice. I had to take jobs, where I left home for several months to make the money we needed. Later on as a family, we traveled the world, had vacations, I bought my daughters cars, and other great gifts over the years. But with all this progress, there were still challenges.

I was grateful that my husband was there for me through most of those challenges. I credit my longtime friends like Laquita, who helped me through my high and low periods.

Let's carry on to Chapter Two so I can talk some mo' about the people who I am grateful for! Ya'll know how I do.

Catching You Up to Date

Melvina W.

The Road is Not Always Easy

Some things can get lost in the path like Friendships.

I would never tell the world I made it on my own. I am quick to point to my husband, Glenn. I also have to include my friends. When I was growing up, having real quality friends was how I coped with issues of being bullied and made fun of on a regular basis. It is good for your heart and self-esteem to know that you are good enough as you are.

The truth is that it takes time to get to know yourself. Seeing yourself through other people's eyes is a great way of knowing how you are perceived. We may think we are friendly when, in fact, we may not be. We can think we can sing, hell, like many people on TV, but we cannot. Who should tell you the truth? Your real friends!

Not everyone is your friend. There will always be people who are like a snake in the grass, and they are around you to mooch off you or see an opportunity to strike at you when you are down. These are not friends.

The Road Is Not Always Easy

Friends don't intentionally try to harm you or lie to you for their own benefit.

Users were amongst the people who said they liked me. Some just wanted money, others your time. Too many people are your friends until the next thing smokin' comes along. You have to test your relationships to know what kind of friendship you have. I don't mean you have to go around putting pressure on people, but you have to allow people to be themselves.

When you see people clearly don't doubt what you see. Sometimes, we want to think people are not as bad as we think they are. We can want something so badly that we blind ourselves to the truth. I tried not to be that way. I believed people when they showed me the good and the not-so-good. Nobody is perfect, but the heart of someone is what you focus on.

When we first met, we were at Devry University in computer programming class, and I sat right beside her, coming into class late. I could not hear the teacher due to my hearing loss, and I remember the teacher pairing us to do a project. Laquita always had a loving heart and would help anyone who needed it. She is a giver, and we connected because deep down, well deep, deep down, I am also. She was the one helping me to figure things out when I first started. If it had not been for her telling me what the teacher said, I would have struggled, as in failed.

You see, sometimes we struggle in life, not because we are not smart enough or didn't try. In my case, I couldn't hear! So, finding a way to win with my

Melvina W.

My best friend, Laquita, has been a ride-or-die friend for many years. We became friends in college and are still friends today.

LaQuita Watson-Parks

Melvina is definitely a risk-taker. She and I have so much in common and I have enjoyed our friendship over the years. It was crazy that when we lost touch, we bumped into each other again at Walmart.

Our friendship has definitely been tested over the years. I can say that I am honest with Melvina when I agree or disagree. She has a dominant voice, and she is not shy. I love her bold personality, and if you hang out with her, you are bound to have a great time.

Going traveling with her was too much fun. She is bubbly and loud but has a heart of gold. She is good at what she does, and I cannot knock her hustle.

We are not twins in personality—I am more cautious than she is—but we do have many similarities, and I believe that is what has made us such good friends over the years.

If anyone wants to learn medical coding, she can tech you and show you her way of doing it, which has worked for her.

challenge was plan number one. If you have learning disabilities or personal hang-ups that pose a risk to you achieving your goals, find a way to work through it.

Find a Laquita or someone willing to help guide you through the material. Get a tutor and study buddy so you know you are digesting the material well. She and I exchanged numbers, and we stayed in touch throughout our college years. We graduated from Devry in 2000 with a Bachelor's Degree in Computer Information Systems.

After school, Laquita did a bridge program to obtain her Master's degree in project management within a year from Keller Management School. I went to the University of Phoenix here in Atlanta for my Master's in Business Administration. We lost touch for some time and ended up meeting again by happenstance at a Walmart!

We were both married in 1998. We both had our Master's degrees and needed a job! We connected on so many levels about how we wanted to move forward in our careers. We do have two different approaches, though, and we learned from each other as we hit the pavement to network and obtain a job.

Personalities will always have dissimilarities. Like any healthy relationship, our relationship has had ups and downs. Through it all, I know she loves me, and I love her dearly. We don't always have to agree or do things the same way. We take a different approach when communicating, for sure, and I am grateful that we don't allow that to tear us apart.

Melvina W.

Not everyone in your life is a "yes" man or woman for you. You want people who are comfortable speaking their minds to you even if you disagree. What if you are wrong about something? I am seldom wrong, but you know that happens like when a total solar eclipse happens. They occur once every three hundred and sixty years–but they happen!

I kid, but in all seriousness, I credit my friendships to hold value in my life–not so much for my business but for personal well-being. Not everything has to amount to dollars and cents. Shocking, I know, coming from the money lady. One of our many differences is I am a risk taker, and I step out on faith. I will jump in deep and she is more cautious. I am more direct, and to me, Laquita can be more delicate with words.

Like my other best friend, Lanett, who is from our hometown, Savannah, I have known her since elementary school. She operates differently than me by being more reserved and humble, while I am essentially the wildcatter and social butterfly. But we most definitely have a lot of things in common, like shopping, traveling, and how we treat people and raise our children. She is extremely wise and smart. But she plays it safe like Laquita--both of them, Laquita and Lanett, are my angels, sweethearts, and very caring gems. There is something about these 'L' names…because there are more Lakeshias, Laquans, etc, who have become close friends, even Dr. Lee!

With any good friendship, you do have to have something–and I would say many things in common. The two of them may differ in personalities, but we be-

The Road Is Not Always Easy

Lanett Thomas

My fondest memory of Melvina and me is our first meeting in 5th grade in Ms. Dilworth's class. I was new to the school, and before my arrival, Melvina was known as the girl with the longest hair and ponytails—that's until I got there (smile). We bonded over our hair and have had "Peanut (Melvina) and Jelly (Me, Lanett)" ever since—knee-high socks and Ponytails.

I can say that I've learned from her to never give up. Whatever you dream can come true through hard work, drive, and perseverance.

She's an inspiration from her beginning and the roller coaster path of her life to where she is now. She continues to thrive for even more success. Come Hell or High Water, the best of her is yet to come.

Melvina W.

lieve in having a nuclear family. We are loyal, dependable, and hardworking. I know her values and mine are also the same. We want to achieve great things in life. I don't recommend hanging around people who don't want anything if you do. They can tend to wear you down or make you feel bad about your own progress.

Laquita and I hit it off so well because we both wanted to be married, have our children, make money, and buy houses and cars while keeping our family together. It was easy for us to lean on each other through our life events because we wanted the same things in life. I remember when we first met, and I was joking with her. I asked her, "Hey, what's your name? I am Melvina?"

Honestly, I couldn't remember her name and was loud when I asked her jokingly, "What's your name again, Laquita?" She would always respond and loosen up a bit. She was a quiet mouse, not saying much, and I guess that is expected of most computer nerds.

From then on, we grew close and started looking for jobs together after completing college. We had no cell phones and technology like today. We quickly understood the value of networking and knew how to talk to people. We had different cover letters but similar resumes and the guts to pass them out. We didn't sit at home sending out inquiries and filling out applications. I love that about us today, by the way.

We would get out there and knock on doors. We showed up to places without appointments and tried to apply for jobs. We had to hustle and present ourselves through rejections. Nothing feels better when you have a long day than coming home and being able to talk it out with a friend who is going through a similar situation. You can lean on each other for encouragement. We grew together.

Same with Lanett, I met her in 5th or 6th grade when I asked who she was. She told me, and when she asked me, I said, "Girl, I was being funny, of course." But from then on, I knew Lanett. We went to middle and high school together and always knew each other. But she had her click of friends, and I had mine. We did not grow close until our adult years when we were both married with children. She has two sons and is now divorced. But make no mistake, she is making boss moves just like Laquita. She is in the accounting field and is a homeowner.

For all of my friends, when finding our husbands, we could lean on each other to weed out the guys who would not fit the bill. We are grown, so the ultimate decision was our own. However, having someone in my corner to remind me of my values, goals, and what I want for my life helps. We can all be caught up in a smoke screen because we want something so badly. It takes a friend to help you see where you could improve and how a love match is a mixed match.

Laquita and I had our children at similar times, and it was also a cherished event for us. We both had all-girls and funny thing. She found out she was pregnant and I joked and said she was having twins. Boom! I called it, and she copied me. She had a pair of girls.

Melvina W.

Dr. Krystal Lee

I met Melvina at an Expo in Atlanta. I don't know a stranger like her. She was passing me, and she offered to support a cause, buying books to support a literacy program with TUG Outreach Inc. (501 C). We chatted for a good minute until she had to find her driver. I loved her soul and spirit, and I wanted to give back to her. I ended up working with her to publish her books, launch businesses, and more.

She is more than a client to me. I feel like we have known each other for longer than a year. We are a lot like each other when it comes to work ethic, values, and being unapologetically you.

What she can teach others is how to code, for sure, but also how to have a mindset to win in any business or life goal. I love how funny she is. I can't help but laugh when we talk, and my tears of laughter from something she said are Real.

The Road Is Not Always Easy

We knew that after graduation, we would have to go back to school to get our masters. We quickly realized that our initial degree was not going to help us earn the money we wanted. She and I wanted to be top earners, and that required more education. We both had families to care for while going back to school and navigating the corporate world. Again, I took more risks, and it paid off.

We were both making good money, but I wanted more in some areas. Besides Laquita, I have outpaced most of my friends in the financial sector. This didn't change my relationship with Laquita, but it did change many of my other friends. I think as you start to excel financially and even in education, your answers to questions and problems can be off-putting to some people. If someone told me something they were thinking about doing that I had already done, I would naturally offer my experience to help them.

Not everyone wants your advice, though. Some don't want to learn from you what could benefit them because they are content with where they are. For my family, I have taken care of financial advancements for the future. I have a beautiful home paid off and working on the second. Glenn has a home that has paid off as well. We are landlords and use our money responsibly. Naturally, when people say they want to buy their second home, for example, I would suggest using the rent from the first house to pay for the second.

For people who can't or won't do that, what I have to say can bother them. At times, you may want to plan a trip or do something. You might have your money, but if they don't have theirs, you can feel funny about having to front the bill for them to go with you. It can become a challenge if you have friends who are not financially where you are.

I can recall taking a trip. Now, if you know me, you know I have a driver. I love Noel; he is great at getting me where I need to go. I trust him to be on time and to be flexible with my schedule. On one of our girl's trips, my friend asked if my driver could take her somewhere. I replied, "Yeah, he can take you where you want to go. Just pay him to get you there." She looked taken aback to find out she had to pay for him to take her somewhere.

Yes, I have a driver that takes me where I ask him to take me. But this isn't a freebie; this is business, and I am paying him to cater to me. Not my friends and family, but me. So, if I want to go somewhere, you can catch a ride with me–if I want you close to me. Or, I will tell you to take your own car if I need some quiet. Sometimes, I have to work in the back of the car, and I don't want to feel like I have to entertain when there is business to get done.

Noel knows me, and he respects me as a client, and I believe he's a friend, too. True friends allow you to set boundaries, and they don't try to force your walls down. They instead grow to respect them. To be fair, some friends you won't mind going the extra mile for when you know their friendship is genuine. People who give you love and think about you, you don't mind paying and doing for them. But I don't believe a relationship should be one-sided.

The Road Is Not Always Easy

Lakeshesia Goolsby

I met Melvina 20 years ago at Medical Coding School. I can still remember the day, and every time I do, I just start laughing so hard. Our teacher had us go around and introduce ourselves and tell her something about us. Once all the introductions were over, we all just started talking about our lives, our spouses, and all. Melvina, being the person she is, started talking about whipped cream and peaches, which were all related to her husband. We all just died laughing. She wasn't shy at all. None of us could stop laughing, including Nicole, our teacher.

We exchanged numbers and became best friends from that day on! Just a quick history. I was an Army wife for 35 years. Melvina showed up to the birthday party with her children and surprised me. OMG!! I was in tears. I really appreciated the support and her driving all that way to be there for me and my girls.

Melvina W.

I have learned that working hard in everything you want, no matter what it is, you have to put the work into it. You must strive to be the best of the best. Everything is possible, and you can achieve anything no matter what it is, regardless if you have children, a spouse, or whatever the circumstances are. She taught me to always fight and never give up on anything.

What Melvina can teach others is definitely a book in my opinion. Wow, to try to sum this up. The first and foremost thing she will teach others is how to work hard and never give up no matter what you are faced with in life. Strive to be the best person that you can be. Never give up on anything. When one door closes, another one opens. Go after your goals and always aim for the best. Melvina will teach others to overcome important sacrifices, live life to the fullest, dream big, and go after their dreams.

The Road Is Not Always Easy

Any relationship worth having shouldn't be one-sided. My marriage requires us both to give. As a mother, I expect a return from my daughters. I don't make any apologies for demanding what I send out to be returned. Of course, people can choose not to give you the same respect you give them. And at that moment, you need to decide whether you want to continue that relationship. You should not be giving two hundred percent, and the other person is given five. Or, as I say, their butt for you to kiss.

As an adult, you have to learn to weigh the importance of your relationships and park people where they need to be in your life. Not every friend is a best friend. Some friends are close for a season, a reason, while others will be there for a lifetime. Some people are going to want different things and have different priorities. Respect them.

What I will say about friendships, you need them like you need family. We all need people in our corner to cheer us on and encourage us as we transition through life. Having people around you who are like-minded will also put a fire underneath you that you need to make something happen. Lifetime friends can love you no matter your successes or failures. Like I said, others can be in your life for an uplifting reason or a season. Don't grow bitter if they leave; some people just gotta go!

Not everyone can go where you are going. I like flying first class, but I have friends who are cool flying coach. I have friends who won't fly at all because of their disinterest or their finances can't afford it. That doesn't mean you can't be friends with people of various backgrounds. This means that your inner circle can be smaller than your outer circle because not everyone can go where you want to go. That relationship might want you to chip in to keep them involved, or you have to put limits on how you befriend the person.

Some relationships I have are on the phone; some are local, and then I have friends who can go toe to toe with me and travel, too. I encourage you to go deep down as you look at your friends to see how they can roll with you. Like Ludacris ' song says, I am going a hundred miles an hour down the highway. If you doing the speed limit, "get —- out of MY way." That simply means I will pass by some of my friends in certain areas because of my expectations.

If you have friends who are doing things you don't do, like illicit drugs, or have other negative behavioral habits, limit your connection with them. Remove yourself if you find they only distract you from achieving your goals. Holding on to dead weight will have you sink faster than making any mistake. Why should you fail because of someone else's life choice? Let them choose how they want to live, and you do the same. "Let it Go!" if you need to. Did I tell you that this is the next book? Let's carry on!

The Road Is Not Always Easy

There are Challenges with Marriage

Communication, growth, and balancing are important for staying a unit.

Glenn and I have been at this marriage thing going on for almost 30 years. Every day hasn't been roses, but our love has grown and deepened over the years. One thing you will notice about me is that when I am committed and set my mind on something, I will accomplish it. Come Hell or High Water! Let me tell you, both single-minded and married-minded people will come your way. Choose wisely if you want to stay married.

Marriage is teamwork, and we both have to keep up our part. Marriage doesn't mean we stop being human, get bored, and let the fire burn out between us because we are stuck with each other. Ironically, I let my marriage help me be free to be me. I don't have pressure from Glenn to lose weight or to be someone I have never been; I can unapologetically be me. I know I

There Are Challenges With Marriage

can be a lot, but for Glenn, I am the right stuff.

When you are looking for your spouse, you have to find someone who accepts you as you are, for better or worse. To be honest, I have picked up a few pounds since I got married, but I am blessed to say our connection hasn't changed at all because of that. Many don't have love like mine, and it is sad. Yes, marriage is a union found on conditions for Glenn and me. In that, we both said we would remain faithful and committed to each other. We respect one another and have never cussed each other out in all our years.

When we are mad, we talk it out, and all the talks are not easy, let me tell you. What we have learned to do is keep open communication. My first piece of advice for any woman–or anybody who wants to have a loving marriage—is to be honest about what you need in a relationship. If you read the first book, you would learn that Glenn and I started dating after a mutual friend of ours said he was not interested in me.

The funny thing is that my mutual friend and I had been dating for years, and I knew it wouldn't go to marriage. So when he indicated that to me one day, I knew it was the nail in the coffin for that relationship. Glenn and I became good friends long before I thought about dating him. To be clear, I think Glenn always had the hots for me, and I had to come to that idea because I was unaware that he liked me in that way.

We were both nerds, and we talked about computers and technology. We studied together, got food a lot, and just enjoyed each other's company. One day, a gentle pillow fight turned into a makeout session, and that's when I found out that Glenn and I had passion. He was an excellent kisser, which is probably why I can't keep my lips off him. He makes loving him easy because he understands me and allows me to be me!

You want a husband who can understand who you are and love you through your strengths and flaws. Glenn doesn't talk nearly as much as I do. I think that is the norm for most women. So we are naturally going to talk, but you want a husband who is actively listening to what you have to say. Nothing is worse than pouring your heart out to someone who isn't listening to you. I am vocal about everything that matters to me, from sexual requirements to emotional, physical, and even the food I want to eat. Especially the sexual requirements… hmmm!!

With Glenn, it was hard to grow in my career because it required me to work remotely sometimes. I remember taking a job for a year in a different state. That was brutal on our marriage. We survived because our communication didn't change even with the distance. Our longing for each other didn't dwindle a bit, either. Too many nights, I felt lonely without him, and the best thing about that was I told him when I missed him and if I needed some goodies.

He wasn't shy either, and some of the best times we have had were after we had been apart for a long while. I remember one time I was so sad. He could hear it in my voice. He tried to be encouraging because we didn't have money then like we do now. So it just seemed right to tough it out. On this day, I didn't care

There Are Challenges With Marriage

The funny thing is that my mutual friend and I had been dating for years, and I knew it wouldn't go to marriage. So when he indicated that to me one day, I knew it was the nail in the coffin for that relationship. Glenn and I became good friends long before I thought about dating him. To be clear, I think Glenn always had the hots for me, and I had to come to that idea because I was unaware that he liked me in that way.

what the cost was to see him; I needed him. I remember telling him, "I need you right now, Glenn." It was like before I could put the phone down, this man got into the car and drove all night to reach me–you hear me?

He came to the hotel at like 4:00 am, and with one eye barely open, I said, "Glenn, is that you?" And almost like a movie, he said, "Yeah, Boo. It's me." I heard his voice, and my eyes were still adjusting from waking out of dead sleep. But within the next blink, I saw my husband approaching me, ready to go, and we enjoyed each other's company for those three days. I left that weekend with the biggest smile on my face, and that was one of the best escapades we had had up to that point. Shhh, listen, those orgasms were so powerful!! I told y'all *I didn't say it was over*!

I guess time and distance do make the heart grow fonder. Moments like that kept us on fire for each other, even with the phone arguments. Yes, phone sex was part of the process, but the best glue to keep us going was communication and being there for each other. I know it took a lot for Glenn to care for the girls, work his job, and manage the house himself while I was gone. I know it was hard on our daughters, too. I will talk more about raising children as you are building in the next chapter, so let's keep this thing going.

Some people might think it is selfish for a spouse to work away from the home–especially for a mother. I have to tell you; I have zero regrets for providing for my family. To the many who may feel guilty driving trucks, working overnights, or doing what you all need to do to make ends meet for a season, remem-

There Are Challenges With Marriage

ber that this, too, shall pass. When I couldn't take being away from my family anymore I quit that job, but not until it afforded me what I needed to provide for my family.

I know Glenn and I are not the traditional couple. We had to find a way to make it work for us. We had challenges other than missing each other and working in different locations. My personality, as you can imagine, is an abundance mindset. I am a risk taker. I am ready to jump when a good opportunity comes around. I have always been a go-getter, and my expectations are high. I want first-class travel, family trips to other countries, and nice hotel stays.

All of those things cost money. I don't have a scarcity mindset. My husband is more frugal than I am for certain things. He likes vacationing, but his version is not the same as mine. At times, that was a problem in our marriage. I wanted things, and it required working good-paying jobs to afford them. My husband is not as big on planning things as I am, either. He is a wonderful provider and takes care of the home, but he wasn't as avid in pursuing big projects as me.

He would be okay with waiting on things, whereas I feel like "Time waits on no man. Time will keep going on until it stops." Why should I stop when I can put my feet on the gas and get on down the road to accomplish what I set out to do? A lot of the success I have accomplished in my career, businesses, and finances was because of my mindset of going after what I could while I could. If there was a way for me to make my desires a reality, I wasn't settling for a dream.

Melvina W.

We talked about going to Africa, and I made it happen. It took years to do it because I wanted to go first class and experience all that I could. I wanted my family to be there, children and all to enjoy the experience. That's without having to imagine looking at a credit card statement and asking, "So how are we going to pay for this?" It was already worked out.

I remember when our eldest child turned sixteen. I thought of getting her a car. I have always been a big giver, whereas my husband has had a different view. I suggested that we get her a five thousand dollar car for her birthday, nothing big. I pulled the money out of my bank account, and I remember him saying nothing while I was doing it. I got to the dealership and paid for the car we selected. I asked Glenn, "So how come you didn't have your half on the car?"

He replied, "You didn't give me enough time to do anything. You just sprang this up on me and expected me to be ready." I replied, "We knew for sixteen years this day would come. I was ready, and you should be too!" He didn't say anything after that. You could hear a pin drop–do you hear me? My husband, when he is processing a talk we've had–or hearing Melvina give her "bitchin" session- grows very quiet.

I guess there really wasn't a right answer at the time. This wasn't a dig at Glenn, but it is an example of how we think. I know he had the money, so that's not it. He sees money differently than I do–and likely because a car is just a car to him. In the eyes of Melvina, I want a driver to drive me in their car. Glenn is content with driving our car.

There Are Challenges With Marriage

I remember I surprised him for his 50th birthday with a trip to Australia! I had to tell him where we were going, but I didn't tell him how I was rolling out the carpet for me. My husband and I have no secrets. We both know what our bank figures are, and we are very transparent about that. But we believe in having access to money and assets of our own.

So when I booked the trip for him, he was expecting to drive us to the airport. The bags were packed, and I was stalling for us to load the car. "Come on now, Marie. We need to get these bags in the car and get going so we won't be late." I replied casually, "Yeah, Glenn. I am almost done. I just need to do one more thing."

Not a moment too soon, up drives our driver, Noel, down our driveway. He pulls up in his nice vehicle and parks. He approached the front door, and I said, "Glenn, you gotta move out the man's way so he can get our bags."

He looked at me and said, "Oh, we are traveling like this?" I replied, "Yes, how else are we going to get to Australia? You thought you were driving? No baby, I got you. Let's get in the car." We had so much fun, and I enjoyed spoiling my husband. I like getting what I like and don't mind the expense–if it is what I want. I know things worth getting and having will cost you money.

My husband grew up in a household a little different from mine, learning how to make it happen with less. That scarcity mindset shows up in how he runs a house. He would shop for generic brands for

Melvina W.

There Are Challenges With Marriage

things when I would sometimes prefer branded items. He would try to save toilet tissue. I say, "If it is there, use it." Those simple things can blow up into big issues when the circumstances are different.

Learning from your spouse is crucial to your career growth if you want to remain married. The two of you are a team, so understanding each other is key to staying together and being a unit. I was glad that Glenn and I didn't have the same level of ambition. I wanted four degrees for myself. I wanted to take my education seriously my whole life. I needed a husband who could understand my mindset and appreciate my plan.

My roadmap included no sleep, working overnights, and skipping things like the gym to work. I had to cut down on things I needed, like eating healthy, going to the gym, and doing things for me to work. My ambitious mindset has proven to be a challenge when it comes to how I treat myself. I know it is a matter of what is important to me. It will become one when I set my mind on it being a priority.

I didn't say it was over because I still have a growth process. We had to maneuver and find a way for Glenn's weaknesses and mine not to separate us but to bring us together. We have to allow each other to be who we want to be. Instead of Glenn fighting me on working from home, going back to school, and getting the things I wanted, he got on board. We found a way to make both of our dreams our dreams.

I wanted to include this chapter in the book because family and spouses are important. I work with

Melvina W.

a lot of women, specifically women in medical coding, and this industry can have some long days. It can be demanding on your time, so you have to find a way to stay connected. I will tell anyone to work and make money but don't forget to flirt with your spouse.

Never stop dating and showing each other attention. Get Disco lights and things to make the romantic life exciting and new. As the years go by, doing the same old thing might not keep the fire lit. So be open to trying things and having fun. You are married! I try to keep the weekends reserved for my husband and family. I can work long hours Monday through Friday, but I will still squeeze time in to give him affection.

No one wants to feel forgotten. Do nice things for each other that are unexpected. Women like flowers, and men like gifts too. Find out what your spouse likes and give it to them to show you care. We both work from home, so it takes a minute to say, "Hey, I love you," or give him a kiss.

I think it is also good to respect each other's space and give each other room to manage things their way. Glenn likes to fix things, and I don't. We both contribute to the bills, so we can feel like a partnership. We kept date night alive, like I said, on the weekends. But you know that isn't enough. Sometimes, you have to get away.

I remember my favorite date night with Glenn; it was a trip we took together to Africa. We went on an African Safari, y'all. We were out there with the animals looking like Adam and Eve. We had an all-inclusive stay and enjoyed drinks, food, water, and Netflix. Y'all know, given that we had a quiet room and we were in a beautiful place, how we spent most of those nights, wink, wink. When we were state-side, we would go to concerts together, sing songs on our way home, and just enjoy our time together.

Sometimes it doesn't have to be going anywhere but sitting on the couch together watching TV. Call that the proverbial staycation. Keep the love by keeping the touching going. You should hold hands, rub each other's shoulders, head or compliment each other. You both have to chase each other. I love that my husband chases me. His compliments and pursuit of me make me love him all over again.

I don't feel like my body is all that great, but he loves it. I feel like my ass could use a lift and a bit more oomph, but he loves it and chases behind me. I laugh as I enjoy every moment of it. If you are having turbulence at home, you have to address it. You have to use your voice. You need to speak up in the medical coding field and in life. My last book in this series talks about letting things go and how I am determined to do that as my career and relationships have evolved.

I do think you need to analyze your relationships and commitments. You must know if you are not comfortable and confident in what you want, it will be hard for anyone to meet your needs. You need to be as close to a hundred percent confident for what you want so the right people can come to you. Marriage is a partnership, and it is not made with one active person and the other person just holding on. I have a lot more

Melvina W.

to say because it is not over.

From my experience, if you want to stay married as you grow in your career, you want to stay calm and not get angry so easily. Men are simple. They enjoy physical touch, quality time, and food. I am the one who needs communication, gifts, words of affirmation, and stuff like that. You don't want to work long hours and fight all the time. It puts a lot of pressure on your marriage and can complicate your plans.

In marriage, I have seen many homes fall apart because people's priorities are different. I know people who make $200k a year and can't travel anywhere. They have nice things, but they have nothing in common with each other. They look rich, but they are emotionally poor. You want to look at how you see savings and future investments and get educated as to how to manage them properly.

In any relationship, both parties need to be able to listen to each other. You need to hear him out and learn what he needs. Then, meet him there and provide for what he needs. You may have to help him in areas that matter to you. If you want him to change clothes or help with the children, you need to speak up about your needs. If you want a 50/50 structure in your marriage, speak up early so you are not bitter toward the relationship.

To improve your family dynamics, you need to speak your heart and mind. Be patient with them. You might have to repeat what you need and put out what you want to come back to you. Support is the best gift

There Are Challenges With Marriage

of marriage, and this is why I believe in it. I would tell anyone to get married because it is a powerful union that aids career success.

My husband has been vital to my success, and without him, I would have stalled in my career. He was my biggest supporter and cheerleader. His support helped me have a clear mind when pursuing my career ambitions. He has supported me monetarily when I needed it. He cleared the path so I could go that "hundred miles on the highway, knocking everyone out of my way," and I thank him for it.

> *I'm Going a 100 Miles down the Highway!*
>
> He cleared the path so I could go that "hundred miles on the highway, knocking everyone out of my way," and I thank him for it.

I thank him for allowing our marriage to be a true partnership in making decisions. When I chose to take an away job, we both came up with the plan to make that happen. Neither one of us unilaterally made plans without communicating with each other. I think more couples need to make plans together and make decisions if they want to last the long haul. Whoever brings up the idea, should also drive the idea. This way, both parties can take turns and feel fulfilled.

Melvina W.

There Are Challenges With Marriage

Sometimes, the one who takes the lead doesn't do everything right. I remember Glenn planned a park trip to Disney World. I got the tickets, and he was getting the hotel. He found a deal; it was $30 a night. I said okay, $30 a night we can save money sounds good.

Turns out, it was a low-end hotel that was renamed. It was a roach motel, and we were all stuck in a room with two beds and a single bathroom. The room was a mess. We encountered one problem after another on our trip to Disney World.

We hated his decision. The hotel stank, and I was fuming. I said to Glenn, "How did you find this hotel?" He said he found it online but never looked up pictures or anything. That would have been the additional homework I would have done. We had to make it work because we were low on funds, and we couldn't shift around. We were on a budget, and it was a rough journey for the family–but we did it. Our marriage was not always perfect; we had some rainy days, too!

I remember telling Glenn to attend school and try to save some money. He could have saved money for things like better lodging for Disney if he had listened to me. He chose to do his own thing in his no-frills way, and I let him do it his way. I told him to start saving back in 2010.

He said he wanted to pay off the credit card balance and stay at the school he picked. It took him until 2024 to pay it off and get the degree. I had to sit and chill on this one because that was his choice. But I still had to bitch for a little bit because it could have been done better.

I do think there should be some ground rules in a marriage–or at least there are with Glenn and me. As a medical coder, I had to have my house in order. We had to be organized and understand our roles. You have to do what you say. Be reliable and responsible. That's in addition to what I said earlier about no cheating and cussing each other out, etc. If you want to grow in your career like I did as a medical coder, you need to be able to shut down so you can work. You have to set boundaries so you can get your work done.

To conclude this chapter before we move on, I suggest having some ground rules to protect your marriage and keep the peace. Don't go to atmospheres that put you in places to step out on your marriage. Don't be a heavy drinker or use drugs to where you are not in your right mind. Don't ever hit each other. Choose your arguments and don't push buttons, which could be avoided.

Lastly, keep people out of your marriage for what works for y'all. Everybody has ideas, but no one is going home with you guys but the two of you. So, do you.

There Are Challenges With Marriage

Melvina W.

There Can Be Backfire

Expect it when you are reaching your goals.

Glenn and I were at peace in the valley. Although we had different ideas for upbringing and raising our daughters, we had to learn to work together. As you can imagine, with my personality, I know what I want. I want my daughters to be strong and independent, value a traditional family, and believe in education.

It is a good thing when you and your spouse can agree on the core aspects of raising children so that you can both enjoy becoming parents without the pressure and noise. When I first got word that I would become a mother, and Glenn a father, we were shocked, and our emotions transitioned into being ecstatic.

The makings of our first child was new love. Glenn and I most definitely enjoyed getting to know each other's sexual preferences, the dos and don'ts, etc. Getting pregnant was indeed an oops situation that wasn't planned at all. I believe Glenn said he was going

There Can Be Backfire
to pull out.

So, our oldest daughter is proof that it didn't work, haha. I remember thinking my period hadn't been on in a while. I didn't think much of it because I thought we were being careful, you know. We played a rhythm game, and we lost.

I took that pregnancy test, and not even a minute later, boop! It said we were pregnant! I was twenty-four years old. Glenn and I were living together in the house I had bought, but we hadn't talked about marriage officially.

At first, I contemplated getting an abortion, but a second later, that went out of the window. I didn't believe in it, and it wasn't a real option; I just feared talking. I told Glenn, "Welp, looks like we are going to have a baby together."

Our firstborn was born with us having a family friend recording on a video recorder her vaginal birth, no pain meds or anything! In the delivery room was my mother, my best friend at that time, and, of course, Glenn watching. Talk about pressure! Soon enough, I became a first-time mother and, of course, Glenn, a father! Mariama came out normal, crying and, of course, beautiful as ever, looking like her father to me--with his eyes and fingers for sure.

We had our first child in 1997 and got married in 1998. We wanted another child after we were married, and honestly, I wanted four children. I told Glenn to take advantage of it while I was in the baby-making

Melvina W.

Mariama Feaster Precious

I love my mom, and I thank her for everything she has done for me throughout the years. As a successful meteorologist and college-educated woman, I have been very blessed to have a good life with my parents.

There Can Be Backfire

business because the shop wouldn't always be open. I didn't want to have my children too far apart. If the next child was a boy, I would settle for a boy and a girl; Glenn didn't care either way.

I replied and said, "See two, what? Two legs?" I was sitting there like a dummy, lost on what she was trying to say. I was a deer in the headlights when she said it again, "I see two babies. Have you felt differently about this pregnancy at all?" I didn't feel any difference. They sent me for another review by another technician to confirm what the first thought she saw.

When I told Glenn, he was floored, shocked, and didn't even believe me. We both went to the doctor the next time, and it was confirmed with him there! Hahahaha!! It was a shocker to be pregnant with twins, geesshhh!!

Sure enough, they were telling us we were having twins. I was overjoyed because I believed God wouldn't give us something we could not handle. I am not overly religious, but somebody had jokes, clearly. I wasn't prepared for my oldest. We had to get things together. I remember we had to buy a lot of baby stuff, and we had our baby shower at my job; then, I was waitressing for the infamous Club 112.

We had to prepare our mindset to be parents for the first go-round, and the second pregnancy had some learning curves, too. We found out about the twins in the second month, so it was early enough for us to buy everything we needed. Even from what we had already, we still had to go out and buy more and double some

Melvina W.

things. Both of my pregnancies were healthy, and I didn't gain much weight, but I lost weight. Ironically, after the children, I gained the weight I lost when pregnant.

We didn't live close to our parents, so we didn't have as much of their support when our children were babies. As they grew older and were all toddlers, we could leave them with my parents for two to three weeks. We turned those weeks into our vacation time. We still had to find time for ourselves because we didn't have a big wedding. We got married at the courthouse. So when my parents watched our oldest, we went to Jamaica on a late honeymoon.

Glenn and I shared responsibility for the diaper stages and early care of the babies. He didn't complain, and when the twins came, we had to tag team to get everything done. Even with children, you still have to make time to keep your marriage healthy. We still flirted like before, and it was an adjustment for us all to work the girls into our routine–but a welcomed one.

With twins, you would have thought we would have had family volunteering to watch them for us, sending us money here and there, and things like that. We didn't get that support, but had to pay for everything. It was trying for sure to find time to do anything when we had to leave the house. We certainly needed more money, especially if we wanted a life.

Here are some of our earliest Memories of our Daughters

There Can Be Backfire

She walked at like 8 months, and started talking a little later than normal girls her age. When she turned about three or four, especially five years old, we discovered that her cognitive learning skills were different, and something seemed off. The talking was not as big, but her struggling to understand literal and nonliteral phrases was our big red flag.

Like her father, Glenn said, "Come on and jump out the shower,"…and she repeated it, "Jump out the shower." He replied, "Yes, come on, and jump out." She literally jumped out, which resulted in her almost falling down on the wet floor. So, now the questions are swarming around, like what is wrong with our oldest daughter? There seems to be a disconnect. Is something wrong?

Now, keep in mind, three years seems like a long while BUT it really is NOT… Because in the year 2000, I got pregnant with my twins. My oldest daughter was 3 years old at the time. Of course, she was walking, talking, and watching cartoons religiously, getting into stuff like her toys, etc. She saw me pregnant with the twins, and we would tell her two babies were going to come out. She would say, "Two babies are going to come out."

In September 2000, the twins were born via c-sections. They were premature babies eight weeks early; they stayed in the hospital for one month to make sure they got to the required weight. Afterward, when they came home as babies, they would cry when hungry, messing up their diapers, etc…standard baby stuff. But once they became toddlers and started running around getting into everything and their older sister stuff, Mariama would ask, "Where did you get these twins from?"

She would also frequently tell Glenn and I to take them back to the hospital. One time, she said that Glenn told her, "They didn't come from the hospital." So, she said, "Well, where did they come from?" I said to Glenn, "Yeah, Glenn, where did they come from?" We laughed. Glenn told her, "The twins came from mommy and daddy," and that got her mind off the question at that time. Keep in mind she was only like five or six years old.

When our girls were young and growing up, all of their experiences meant the world to us. I remember sitting on the sofa feeding them. They each would lay on my chest, making bubble noises to me–likely trying to talk. I would just find myself looking at them and admiring what Glenn and I had made. It was to each of them that I made a commitment to be the best person/mother I could be for them. They became the WHY for why I did everything and accomplished as much as I have over the years.

One of my fondest memories of my oldest child, which still has me laughing, is I asked her if she wanted some juice. She looked at me and said, "I want some juice, Marieeeee…Marie." I was in tears laughing because she was calling me like how Glenn did and she nailed it. You know I got that baby some juice!

With the twins, Sierra used to eat more than

There Can Be Backfire

Sierra Fenster

Some of my fondest memories with you are from when we spent time watching TV shows and movies together. I remember laughing with you during funny moments and enjoying those simple, shared experiences. Those times made me feel connected to you. I also think about our trips to stores or restaurants—those moments, even if they were routine, felt special because we were spending time together.

You played a strong role in shaping my education. I remember you always being supportive, from helping me with school projects to attending school events. You made sure I had the tools I needed to succeed academically and encouraged me to do well in school, which made me take my studies seriously.

You've been a model of hard work and independence. Watching you juggle your responsibilities showed me how important it is to stay committed and focused, even when things get tough. You've taught me resilience through your actions and provided me with the foundation to handle challenges in life.

Melvina W.

Amira. Sierra used to drink from the bottle and flatten the nipple trying to get all of her milk. I was so tickled to see her face and cheeks. Sierra was quick about walking too. She walked about a month before Amira, and neither one of them were crawlers.

The days I missed sometimes were are when I made king food for them. As toddlers they loved my food and; I didn't have to fight with them to eat. When I would make them a snack, french fries, I would draw their names in the ketchup for dipping; and they thought it was the best thing. I loved seeing their eyes light up for something so seemingly simple. It felt good to provide for them and make them happy.

Alright, let me stop gushing over the baby phase; it's been awhile. The twins were about three years old, running around the house playing… the oldest was is in school, kindergarten. I am at home watching them during the day and at night I go to work the graveyard shift. Afterward, I would come home everyday to care for the twins, while the oldest goes to school.

I picked up the oldest from school everyday. So essentially 9:00 am to 5:00 pm was my shift with the kids and at night my husband watched the girls and put them to bed, etc. So, one particular day, Sierra the oldest twin got her head stuck in the dining room chair… and Amira, the youngest twin ran around the corner yelling, "Sierra stuck, Sierra stuck…come on…"

I got up urgently running around the corner into the dining room and saw her head stuck.I had to slowly

There Can Be Backfire

help her remove her head out of the chair with a little grease and patience to do the trick. Like everything time was carrying on and the twins were getting ready for kindergarten, and doing the preliminary stuff for starting school.

So, after running a vision and hearing test needed for school, we discovered the news of what I had passed down, sorry to say…a nerve loss from birth, to the twins. They were both hearing impaired… like who? Me! Life was beginning to get interesting. Our oldest daughter was now in the 2nd or 3rd grade. Around this same time, her school counselors and teachers called us in to tell us that she has a high-level performing autism called Asperger's syndrome, and that was why she struggled so much socially with her peers.

Other ways we had to support and take care of our daughters were their health concerns. They each were born with a different set of needs. Being a child born with a nerve loss, which cost me 50% of my hearing, I was aware of some of the challenges they would face. I had the heart and mindset to help them. With our three girls, we had to learn to manage Asperger Syndrome, Hearing Loss, Juvenile-Myoclonic Epilepsy, and Tourette's syndrome.

For each daughter, we had to design a specific IEP (Individual Educational Plan). No two daughters were alike in that sense, not even the twins. It takes a village to raise children, and that village doesn't have to be only family members. We had to work with specialists, doctors, their teachers, and service agencies to ensure they got everything they needed. I stayed on top of everybody and made sure that when they went to high school, they were on track to go to college and not get a certificate of completion.

It never was an option for my children to lean on their disabilities as an excuse for under-performing. They needed to learn differently, but they all could learn and achieve success. I had to push and motivate them to strive for greatness because I wanted the same for each of them. Mothers with children who have disabilities still want the same things as parents who have children who do not have special needs.

I made sure that we started applying for their college careers early on. When they were in ninth, tenth, and eleventh grade, I was pushing the doors open for them to go. I made it clear that education is an absolute must, and a bachelor's degree is the starting point. *I didn't say it was over* because of the challenges; we just learned to adapt and learn to carry on.

Teaching them about their bodies was also my job. I remember having to demonstrate what they needed to do for their menstruation with pads and hot sauce so that they wouldn't be embarrassed but prepared. I had the "sex talk" with them and explained how to take care of their bodies. I answered anything they wanted to ask me about point blank so that they would know.

The same way I take care of my children is the same way I care for coders. I know being a baby in coding or wanting to learn a new area, you will have a lot of questions. That doesn't bother me. I know people feel like they have to apologize for the many questions.

There Can Be Backfire

You don't. I want to make sure you know and have everything you need to be successful.

My girls are all successful and high achievers. When I was working and traveling, it was a mental challenge for all of us for ME to be away. I worked away from home and traveled for about two years. Besides that, I have been there with them, pursuing work from home. I was there for a lot of major events in their lives, but unfortunately, I did miss some of them. It pained them and me not to be there for them when they needed me.

Don't get me wrong, I was always a phone call away, but at times, I realized that it felt too far away. I have no regrets, though for what I had to do to provide for my family, but I don't like the strain it put on my relationship with my daughters. I am glad that they got the principles I needed them to learn about their disabilities. My push was to make my children great, and I know that that didn't feel like the best at times, but like tough love is good, it was for their greater good.

As mothers, we cannot always please our children. The truth is we can't please them if doing what is best for them requires a tough decision. Working is a part of life; we must learn to adjust the best way we can. I would admit I am not the perfect mother, yet, I am a damn good one. I provided for my children in every way I could. My heart towards them has never wavered.

I knew that as an adult, my children would all have issues. How do they provide for themselves, pay bills, and take care of things? When they were in college, Glenn and I taught them what they would need. They learned independence from me, but I trust they also know my love. When they arrived at college, I made sure the principal, administrators, teachers, and staff knew how to treat them. I didn't leave their side or stop being their cheerleader–ever. And I still didn't say it was over… I am and always will be their MOTHER! PERIOD!!

I had so much love to give that even after the twins were born. I wanted to try one more time for a son. But the girls were born three years apart, and Glenn pumped the brakes on that. He said, "Babies are expensive." Hahaha. Shortly after that conversation, he got a vasectomy, and my plans started to fade away. I still had a heart to adopt, so to speak, but I ended up "adopting another girl" and never had a son. I guess it just wasn't part of God's plan.

I remember talking to my daughters about college. Some of them wanted to do the cutesy stuff, like hair and art. I told them, "I am not paying $12,000 for no cosmetology license," I knew of too many people struggling to pay their bills with it. I encouraged them to take a different major, like civil engineering, meteorology, and psychology. My "adopted daughter" is studying to be a Registered Nurse. They all have practical skills to work a job and provide for themselves, which was always the plan.

There Can Be Backfire

My Adopted Daughter

Let me take a second to explain this adopted daughter. She is a young lady born and raised in Nairobi, Kenya, in her 20s. Glenn and I met her when we were over there for two weeks to celebrate my birthday. Glenn and I did NOT legally adopt her. She was my personal photographer for the two weeks when we were there.

After communicating with her for a year after Glenn and I returned home, I truly became impressed with her and her drive to succeed despite her limited resources and extremely poor infrastructure in Nairobi, Kenya, compared to the United States of America. Like I told her, if she truly wants Glenn and me parenting her and investing in her like a daughter, let's put it in place and the rest is our story!!

Melvina W.

My Adopted Daughter

She is a full-time student at Daystar University seeking a Bachelor of Science degree in nursing. And if you are wondering why I call her my adopted daughter, it is because I am literally providing all financial assistance for her shelter, education, food, clothes, electronics, even a car, and more. I am now responsible for this young woman to complete her goal and be better than she could have ever dreamed because Glenn and I have claimed it!

There Can Be Backfire

All my daughters went to school because of the ground rules their father and I set. Just like in marriage, with parenting, you have to establish the rules of the house. The first and main one for me is, "I am not your girlfriend, aunt, or grandparent. I am your mother." "What I say goes" and "This is not a democracy." I know those words will probably haunt them now, but when they have children, they will understand. You don't always have time to explain yourself–nor should you try.

I was an old-school momma, and I believe in discipline. I took things away from them, sent them to their rooms (they had their own rooms), and they got light spankings when they were really young. One of my daughters was really smart. So, when we took her technology away, she entertained herself with books!

She loved to read, and that is a good thing, but not when you are on punishment. So, my husband came up with something more creative. He made her write papers on a subject, and it wasn't to check her grammar or anything but to discipline her. She started to groan then. But I firmly believe that boundaries and rules should be followed and enforced because the real world and a job will have rules, too. So you need to know how to work within them. It is a valuable lesson that many teenagers of any ethnicity should learn from their parents.

If I could give my two cents to other mothers, including those in medical coding, I would say that when you establish your boundaries, it is easier to work. When your house runs smoothly, you can focus while

Melvina W.

on a computer and doing what you need to do.

Get involved with their lives and help support them with what they need to succeed so they can give you grace when you need time to work or study. It is hard to teach your children something you don't practice. When I needed time to work, I made it clear that I was studying to learn a new program or system.

I supported whatever they wanted to do as a hobby, but I wasn't going to pay for a college career as a hobby. One of my daughters is talented in creative writing, film, and theater, but her father and I couldn't help her as much in those majors. It was tough. I am sure for her to pursue a different career path at first was difficult, but she saw the big picture. Now, she can pursue her interest in film or creative writing.

I have to be honest; I had a wonderful relationship with my daughters until they started to grow into their own. It is normal for people to think differently, and that causes some friction. I am respectful of our differences. We are working through learning each other now that they are all adults. The more they accomplish in life, the more they will understand me, and perhaps I can see a few things differently.

When we age, we think we will grow to become more wise. Although life changes, one thing won't change: I love my life choices to have and provide for them. I have four degrees and am on the road to publishing three books. I own several businesses, including a medical coding school, and I have had a successful career as a medical coder. However, the best job I have

There Can Be Backfire
is being a wife and mother.

It is my prayer that as my children grow older, we will draw closer. I understand the dynamics have changed with them being adults and will change again someday when they have their own families; that is fine. I do enjoy them, and they were the greatest gifts given to Glenn and me.

Nothing beats the feeling I had knowing I would become a mom–besides my wedding day. After all, he is the reason the days happened, right? In retrospect, if you want to jump-start your career in any field, you can do it even if you have young children. One of the things I stress is teaching your children what you know. I taught my children everything I knew so they could grow in any field.

What I liked about being home was that I could be available to do things they needed me to do. In that, if they needed a conversation, I was home. As they grew older, this field became easier. It can be harder when they are young babies because you cannot break from the traditional job of cooking, cleaning, and picking them up.

So you have to afford to hire help to do those things to help you focus on what is more important. I did meal prep and the laundry on the weekend and got help from my husband and professionals throughout the week. If possible, don't be afraid to pay someone to help you organize things inside your home if that affords you time.

Melvina W.

I would share this to help all mothers: You have to make time for yourself, too. Children are great, but you need to have tenacity and create a world that you can live in. Your children should not be your whole world in that you don't have a life without them.

I know this might be a sore subject for parents and children when they need to get their own place. Knowing when to let your children fly from the nest is an important step in life. They won't be home forever. After they have a college degree and a job or when they don't respect you, it is certainly time for them to move out and get their own nest. With some children, you have to shoo them out regardless of if their clipped wings are ready.

I don't believe a parent should deal with disrespectful adult children when the parent is paying the bills and doing the bulk of the domestic work. It takes money to have opinions and judgments; if you want to pay the cost to be the boss, carry on. So, don't be quick to choose your children over your spouse or let the children become what divides a marriage between the parents.

Keep things good with your spouse. When you are an empty nester like us, you want to still have a marriage. Glenn and I did the work to stay close over the years, and I am glad for itl. We were partners, a team, and we had to agree even if the girls didn't agree with one or both of us.

In a marriage, you need a united front filled with love. We are able to have more fun now that the house

There Can Be Backfire

is empty–for all the right reasons. We love each other very much, still. What I wanted was a career that would take care of Glenn and me, too. We cannot disappear to allow everyone else to live because then we would stop living. You want to strike a balance.

Fun Fact:

Striking a balance, I also have to acknowledge my mother-in-law, who has helped me to become the person I am today. I have had some mother-in-law challenges by marrying her youngest son, Glenn, and her baby. Over time, we have grown to become a family, and I love her dearly. Ironically, her name is the same as my middle name, "Marie."

I often joke with my husband and ask, "Who is your mother, Glenn? Hahahaha! She is an involved grandmother who helped watch her grandchildren from time to time as they grew up. I cannot thank her enough for helping to develop my husband's heart and patience for being surrounded by women. He grew up with his mother as a single parent with two sisters, so he didn't mind being in a house full of women (a wife and three daughters)!

Now, keep reading and see how I came into my own, and you can too!

The Painful Journey with the girls it is not always easy for me to speak about our relationship. I am very forthcoming with my career accomplishments, but as a mother, there has been some turbulence. It might sound strange, but making more money wasn't the fix to all my problems. Money couldn't fix what I had to endure as a mother. It wasn't all peaches and cream over here.

It pained me to see my beautiful children growing up, and I was not able to rid them of the hurt that I caused. I made sacrifices to advance my career throughout the years, which included leaving them with their father. I left every time with tears in my eyes. I questioned my choice and asked myself, why am I

Melvina W.

Amira Fenster

We would travel, go to the movies, and laugh about simple things that made my childhood timeless. It did not have to be worth 1000 dollars as long as I could spend quality time with her. It meant a lot to me as a kid, and I tend to look back at those moments often.

There Can Be Backfire

doing this? OMG!! My choice to prioritize my career and make the money to afford what I knew they needed kind of BACKFIRED in the worst way!

They never had the words to articulate this hurt when it happened. To be fair, maybe I wasn't all ears to hear it either. I knew what I had to do, and as their mother, I had to make a tough choice. I didn't have the option to be at home and work my jobs early on since about 2015, but COVID changed everything in the world–medical coding included.

I had to go out and get it. The words would formulate in their hearts and manifest in their treatment of me. It hurts and stings very badly in my heart. As mothers, we always want to protect our children. I did just that, and I am proud of it, yet in another sense, I feel like I failed, to be honest. (Please know I am in tears as I type this…) And *I didn't say it was over*!

I remember being told that I was a narcissist and a person they don't respect anymore. In many conversations, I told them, "This is not a democracy. This is a straight-up dictatorship in this house. What I say goes…" They would ask, "Does their opinion matter?" I said, "Nope, not up in here; it does NOT!"

They said, "I belittled them because I made them feel like they were less than me." The truth is children don't know what is best for them. They lack the experience to know enough to make grown-up decisions. Especially the decisions I had to make as a grown-up. I want them to understand they don't have to agree with me, but respect and trying to understand me

Melvina W.

is all I can ask for.

My words could have been softer, and I would agree. I love hard. I am bold, a go-getter. It can be hard to turn that off because I am the same every day. And yes, I pretty much concur with that assessment of me. They told me, "Everything is always about money with you, Ma - that is all you think about."

And I said, " Ain't that a blip; you are riding around in a car I bought you! The clothes from Torrid on your back; I bought them! Those cellphones you talk on to call me cruel, I paid for. God only knows what sacrifices I have had to make over the years to provide you with things you wanted and needed. How am I going to pay for these things if I don't work? Who is supposed to get these things for you? Who's responsible?" They said, " That is what you are supposed to do."

So, you see, life doesn't always have easy answers. There is truth in everyone story. If you think my heart was NOT literally bleeding, you are highly mistaken…it was. I paced the floors at night: because I couldn't seem to get a handle on this. I couldn't fix the issue. I am good at problem solving and making things work for others and my job. My marriage is great. Glenn and I have a groove, and we are very happy.

I no longer knew what to do with my daughters, or how to mend this part of our relationship. I love them more than life itself, but they have these feelings towards me because of my actions, my sacrifices that I made--the economic choices I felt were necessary. I know I cannot force a change, we are all grown. I

There Can Be Backfire

would like for them to know my heart, though.

We have to give our children their choice and trust them to see our side and have more understanding. I know that doesn't fix it all, but perhaps if we all respect each other's perspective, we can heal. We are on a healing journey now, and it took time for us to get here. All the kinks are not worked out, but we are better than before. I realized they needed me to be there when I had left to do jobs.

They are crying from within, trying to fight for their own independence. As a mother, I see the shortcomings, and I want to help because I can help them develop with my wisdom. As a mother who has been there and done that, essentially, I am still someone they need now, and I am here. I apologize that I couldn't be there then, but we cannot live in reverse. They could NOT see things through my eyes on the calls; their pain spoke louder in many ways. Some things I have come to realize are embraced later when life has a way of teaching us all!

Finding Your Own Way

The people who become wealthy in any field find what works for them and multiply it.

I am not yet wealthy, but my goal is underway. To me, being wealthy is having half a million dollars coming in monthly without working at all. Yup, passive income is part of the wealth sphere, but that kind of wealth isn't everything. Generational wealth, good health, money, savings, investments, all those things are needed in my opinion to be wealthy.

Currently, I have some of each category, but I haven't maxed it out in the way I want. I still have a ways to go, and I am sure there are things in your life that you can acknowledge you have a ways to go. If you are not making the money you want in the field you are in, you are probably looking at medical coding and questioning how you can get it done.

I will be the first to admit that medical coding has afforded me a wonderful lifestyle in which I have been able to put away money, start my retirement fund,

Finding Your Own Way

and leave a nest egg for my husband and daughters; butI don't believe that's enough with grandchildren to come. Hint hint. So, presumably just like you, I structure ways for how to maximize what I have.

If you want to make it big in any field, you have to find where you can dominate. For some people who play sports, they find where their greatest strength lies, then they build their best game on that ability. Yes, you want to diversify your financial portfolio as such but we find that, ultimately, our best skill to master is how to level up.

You will find that most people who make the most money with one job or career, are hyper-focused on an area. For me that is medical coding! When I learned about my characteristics and how my personality could help me land a successful career in the field, I never looked back. I am punctual, matter-of-fact, and I enjoy studying.

I am driven passionate about making money and living the lifestyle I want. I was too ready to jump in with both feet when I started my first job. It was a task getting through school. However, I will always say it was worth it. I am still learning new ways I can better my skills even now after nearly two decades in this field. I didn't say it was over–instead we have only just begun!

If you want to just have tunnel vision and not develop the tenacity and thick skin you need to become a thousandaire, you haven't been looking at prices. I am not quite a millionaire, but you need to focus on your

Melvina W.

motivators. What are the key aspirations you have to push you?

Have you heard of the saying, "Reach your hands over your head."? The person would likely lift their hands over their head less than their best effort. But if someone held a twenty or hundred dollar bill over their heads and said, "If you can grab it, you can keep it," How many of us could reach further? We would stand on our tiptoes, extend our fingers, and fix our arms so as not to bend at the elbow. Whatever it took to make that extra stretch to grab that money, we would do.

The same is true when it comes down to obtaining what you want in life. You have to be willing to stretch yourself, push, and test the limits of your ability. Of course, something has to be within reach that you want; it helps if you already have the drive to get there. Some people who don't own cars hardly ever think about traveling. People who have little in the bank don't usually think of plans that require money. But when they start wanting things, visualizing what they want and seeing what it takes, that helps expand their dreams.

Finding Your Own Way

For me, the three principles again are family, love, and money. Whenever I looked at my husband, saw my daughters, and thought about the love and family I had, it reinforced my need to acquire money. Not so that I may boast and find my confidence in it but so that I can use those principles to afford what I want. I'm talking about having the ability to impact my family through choice and responsibility. I don't take it lightly to be in a marriage, be a mother, or owning a business, etc. All of the hats I wear carry major responsibility.

I would be the first to admit that I found my strengths by looking at what mattered most to me. When I had a family to fight for, I dug deeper into my gifts more than before. Being a waitress at Club 112, one of the hottest nightclubs at the time, I knew I could work toward becoming one of the best. I learned how to talk to people because people from all walks of life came to the Club to be entertained.

My job then was to make money by ensuring people had a good time with good service; For some of us, social interaction might not be your strong suit. The question I ask my mentoring clients is "Tell me about yourself?" I ask that question because knowing yourself is half of the battle. If you are shy, you want to know what can help you break a little bit from that shell to develop confidence when you communicate with doctors.

Many cognitive doctors and regular people are short on time or impatient; these people tend not to be sensitive with their words. They are pretty direct, say what they mean, and they are expecting you to keep up with the conversation. For people who are soft spoken, it is easy to get lost in the shuffle or simply not be heard because confident and calm personalities tend to do great in the medical field.

If you are rushed into an emergency room (ER) do you want a loved one or an attendant speaking to you softly to where you have to keep saying, "Sorry, I didn't hear what you said. Can you say that again?" How long before someone would likely lose their temper if they are already under stress. Any job can bring on stress, working with confident people makes that job easier. I was never shy about talking. I am loud, confident, and knowledgeable.

Yet, I am not the Energizer Bunny, and I run out of juice like everyone else. You can get burned out in any field if you feel like it's not leading somewhere. As you build for what you want to accomplish, it is easier to get to work. Finding the strength to make it in your field of choice requires you to see your vision and the steps you are taking. Hold on because the start is always bumpy.

When I got my first medical coding job, it wasn't paying but $14 an hour. Although that wasn't a whole lot, it was a start. In college, my goal was to be a computer programmer. I wanted to make 60k to 80k a year, and I thought it would be a blessing if I could reach 100k. This market was very saturated, so I started to expand my vision and include other similar fields.

When we are starting something new, we cannot get intimidated or frustrated with humble beginnings. I took this job and it was nowhere near enough for me to

Finding Your Own Way

Jennifer Nelson-Criss

My fondest memory is the first time I met Melvina; it was at my first Sorority meeting in my new chapter. I did not know anyone, and it was at the end of the meeting. Melvina walked right up to me and introduced herself immediately, asking me about my time in the sorority, family, job etc. She asked me if I was going to an upcoming sorority conference and if I needed a roommate and a ride. She made me feel welcomed, and I knew we immediately we were going to become close friends

Melvina has taught to not limit myself and to think outside the box. I learned how to take risks in my life and career choices. She taught me if you think big it can happen.

Melvina is a great teacher. Her training is tough but her lessons were detailed and I was able to pick up the material very quickly which allowed me to start a job right away. Even though I am not working in coding right now I still use her tips in working in my current job.

meet the demands of a growing family. Glenn and I had to rob Peter to pay Paul, in an effort to stabilize economic demands. We were in school at the same time, so we were growing together, and I was moving a bit faster than him.

I remember we had to make payment arrangements to pay bills. I knew this was me paying my dues so that I could get into a position to make the money I wanted. I didn't let this early start deter me from my goal of making good money as a medical coder. I could see that this was a step on the pyramid to get to the top!

I soon got a second job, and it felt like a good bit of the money went to daycare, but that which money couldn't buy was knowledge. While working at the two jobs, I knew I had to acquire more wisdom to help me earn high-paying jobs. I begin doing what I do best: talking and asking a series of questions.

Even though I can talk, I found the value in listening. I would take people to lunch, ask questions, and listen for their answers. I would start implementing what I heard to see how far I could advance with it. If something didn't work, I would repeat the process.

I didn't skip a networking mixer or anything I could attend to grow my network in the industry. I met with people from the American Academy of Professional Coders (AAPC) and the American Health Information Management Association (AHIMA) to understand more about certifications, expectations, and board discussions. I went to AAPC and AHIMA conferences and other medical coding events. I started to zero in on

Finding Your Own Way

what areas were offered to me. At these events, if there are fifty people there, you need to commit to meeting at least thirty of them or more.

When you go to chapter meetings, ask the questions the employers need to know. When you are in an interview, ask the interviewer questions about the position, the company, and the workload. If you are passed up for a job, ask the bearer of the news why you were passed over. Also, ask what you could have done better. Look to see if there is more you can do or offer in the future for the next position.

You are not going to get to the top sitting on the sidelines. You have to get in the game to start making powerful plays to get noticed. You need to be bold and a risk taker, putting what you want out there. Yes, you study, but you have to start implementing what you are learning, even if you make mistakes on the way. Being the new kid on the block means coming in early and putting in more time and effort than everyone else. I wasn't perfect when I started, but had to build experience.

If I had worked a job for four months, by the time I left, it would have been like I had worked it for four years based on the wealth of understanding I had garnered. I wanted to know how to be a few steps ahead of where I was so that someday I could get to where I wanted to be. I didn't lean on looks and expectations for this industry to make my way. I am dark and a woman with a disability in the South competing for jobs, which statistically were held by white persons. If I can break into an industry and make a name for myself, anyone

Melvina W.

can.

    I say that not to discourage anyone or to cast a cloud over my success. I don't want you to limit your success based on things outside of your control. I share my truth so you know that anyone can do this. I want you to take a moment and assess what you are putting a ot of your time into. How are you spending your time?
    If you are spending a lot of your time watching tv, for example my question is is that helping your goal manifest? If you are doing anything, is that thing you are doing making your goals closer or further away? When I started my career, I had to choose between what I wanted and what I needed to do. What you need to do is not always fun, but it is more profitable in the long run.

    We all have to sow seeds and push ourselves to make life happen. We can sit down and twitter our fingers and say we want more, but if we are not going after it and making ourselves known, we can kiss your future goodbye. It doesn't mean you are not great or that you cannot do it, but it implies that your motivators and your desires simply aren't there. Whatever you want, bad enough, you will go after it and find ways to make it happen.

    I never let my family starve. They meant too much to me, and although I was falling asleep on one job to get to the next, I fought through it to make it to the other side. Yes, I have quit my job and got fired from some. I am not perfect, but I am also not a quitter. I do what I need to do to survive; then, I also learn to thrive. As you adapt to this industry–well, anything,

Finding Your Own Way

you'll learn to work smarter.

    I kept the jobs I wanted because I learned how to nail the job. I was able to grow in this field because I was willing to learn something and learn how to do things better beyond the status quo. Start with an open mind, and don't assume you know everything. This industry is vast, and I am sure as time rolls on, I may obtain another certification.

    I thought about going back to school. Can you imagine it after four degrees? But it is true. If a degree stood in the way for me to become wealthy, you best believe I would find a way to make it happen.

    Prioritizing is important to your growth. It is very important to learn the system codes and not be afraid of formal education advancement. When I had those jobs, new codes were constantly introduced. I learned to master my niche by being keenly proactive.

    I recommend using 3M Encoder, webinars, and doing bits of training on the AHIMA and AAPC websites. When you are getting a new job in coding, especially, pay close attention to everything. Orientation and the videos you have to watch are there for your training. Your boss assumes you have paid attention and will know this material.

    The best time to impress the new company you work for is at the start. If you don't put your best foot forward, there might not be too many more tomorrows. So, take notes, pause the video, give yourself flashcards like when in school, and pay attention as much as you can to new material. Each job I took, I made it my job to learn it through and through.

I make six figures now because I put in the work to learn what everyone around me has to do. I know how the parts fit into each other. Having a good understanding of the big picture helps you to see your job clearly, and the companies need even more so.

If you are on a fast track to make more money, learn everything you can and set a time frame for how long you want to be at the job. Some jobs are not forever, but they are a means to an end. Don't be afraid to work two jobs, especially in the beginning. You can make double the money and get twice the experience.

When I help coders elevate on the job with my mentorship program, I focus on a specialty they need to learn to make more money. Also, what to say and how to function on the job. There are trends in this industry, and I can show you how to apply them to get high-end positions.

Some departments simply pay more money, and oftentimes, coders need to expand to other specialties to make more money. So if you are stuck with a job that has a cap, I can show you how to remove that stumbling block. It is crazy for you to go to coding school and spend ten to twelve thousand dollars and cannot get a job. After hearing that I wanted to find solutions.

The biggest problem is people are not prepared and may not know what to do when they get on the job. I help coders learn their job when they are hired and teach them how to work up the ladder by teaching them new skills. I cannot stress how important it is to have references and resumes built for scenarios. The right resume can help you land the job and not get passed by. Some projects want a short-term and a certain set of experience. I have dumbed down my resume to get a job and scaled my services.

You can put too much on the resume, which can make the hiring director lose sight of what you are applying for. Your cover letter matters, and I help people write and submit their key services to get a job. My focus with most medical coders is to help them get a job. For new coders, it begins with learning to code so they can get a job. I didn't want to have a school that couldn't help people get a job.

My struggle as a new coder was getting and keeping a job. If you are paying for education, you need to make sure your investment will start turning a profit quickly. Especially, if you have loans and things. I personally think you should pay for a cheaper program, so you are not in debt. Most schools charge more than ten thousand to learn this industry. My coding program is 10% of that price and we run special sometimes which offer the program for just under a thousand.

I would suggest looking for a program that will help you get a job and is not so focused on your studying material. What you learn in the books is one thing, but how you can implement that information is everything. For me to really make money in this field, it took practicing it. If you are a licensed coder, you have access to opportunities. With more experience, it opens up more options.

Melvina W.

I have helped six coders break into this industry, making 50K a year or more, who wanted to be featured in this book. I am so proud of them, and they are a testament to the fact that women (most of my students are women) enter this field and do very well. If you are ambitious, you can make six figures a year and afford to provide for your family. Retirement is a real option, and if you are more like me, I can help you see how I am doing it, and you can, too!

You need a strong-will mindset to make it anything because there will always be obstacles, competition, and challenges. Make it your choice that you will win, no matter what is going on or what comes your way. I remember when I took a job for a particular company. The business has been up and running for years, but they have failed to stay up-to-date with Current Procedural Terminology (CPT) and International Classification of Disease 10th Revision (ICD-10) coding guidelines. Some companies out here are making up their own industry rules or using their own mom-and-pop way of coding that will get you fired from any other company.

Such companies have a revolving door of coders because new coders don't understand their format, and their current coders cannot go anywhere because they learned the wrong way. If you find yourself in this situation, I would say run and get help from me or someone else who can help iron out the things you don't know. Of course, the books will help. Use them and check in ever so often to our coding guidelines so you know the changes.

Finding Your Own Way

Jennifer Toussaint

My fondest memory...Wow. There's so many because they are all filled with laughter. I think the funniest memory was when Melvina had a live-in roommate and didn't know it. As I type this, I'm still cracking up about it.

Out of all the nugget of knowledge that I've learned from Melvina, the one most impactful that I live my life by is that life is about options. Stand by your decisions, no matter how good or bad they turn out to be. You always have options to turn things around.

She can teach that "Everyone has excuses, but can you get beyond those excuses to WIN at life?"

Melvina W.

Another job had once told me I would work at 9:00 am. The day of, they called at 8:00 am, then told me I had to have my camera on all day while I worked. I couldn't have a cup on my desk. I couldn't eat while I worked–even though I was expected to work through my lunch if a deadline required it. Needless to say, I was another coder who walked through that revolving door. Some jobs won't work out, and it is not your fault. If you want more freedom, jobs exist that offer it.

If you walk into a company that is backward, not doing things by the book, and is a ticking time bomb, get out of dodge as quickly as possible. Keep looking for other jobs, and don't plan to stay long where the building is on fire. Our coding guidelines are there to regulate our industry. Some companies feel they don't need to apply them, but they do.

Getting your certification implies you are going to follow the rules, and you know them. So protect the education you invest in, and be okay with stepping away from companies that do not value our coding guidelines. They will not help your career advance. While all money is good money to me, not all companies are!

If you get fired, don't let that deflate you. It happens; you win some, and you lose some. But when you are getting your foot in the door, try to keep your job to build your history and experience. When you are new, you don't want to be too quick to close a door. You want to learn how to move on.

As you get new assignments, don't list the jobs

Finding Your Own Way

you were fired from. Don't put jobs on your resumes where you were fired if you don't have to. This is where references will help out. Find people who believe in you and can help you navigate this industry.

So don't quit if you feel like you are doing bad. It happens, and yes, some positions can be a challenge, but hang in there. You can benefit from being laid off or let go.

So, don't send away your benefits because you are afraid of getting fired. If you feel overwhelmed with the workload, do something to clear your mind. If you have a mentor, check in with that person. Get help from others in the industry if something isn't working well. Don't just ignore problems.

I still have mentors who help me with coding. So, if you don't have a person to help you with new codes, get one. There is always something you might not know that you must learn. So, expand the network of people you work with and the people you pay.

I think, too, if you find an area you like, pick people in that industry or that specialty. I don't recommend hard or high-level experience areas out of the gate. Consider the popular, simpler, less experienced type of coding when you start, and then scale up to other fields or other types of coding.

If you need more training after you get a job to make more money, see if the job can pay for you to go back to school for two years. My program is eight weeks long and can help you get a job. But if you want

Melvina W.

to make more money, you might have to go back to school. Don't turn it down if the company is paying for it. This will help increase your value and keep you out of debt all at the same time.

Finding Your Own Way

I Don't Want Peanuts!

I want the whole store! When what you have isn't enough!

If you are okay with making peanuts, you should have stopped reading several chapters back! Haha, but I am checking though; have you been listening? I am money motivated, family oriented, and I have big goals. I am bold, brave and a risk taker. Don't you know this is the recipe for an entrepreneur and a person who wants to make more and have more in life?

You don't have to give up your belief to want to make money and provide for your family. I am not the person who will associate poverty with believing in God and living a good life. Too many people are focused on doing what others say is the right thing instead of what they need and want. I want to tell you, you can have what you say!

I said when I was thirteen I would have a maid, and I do! I wanted to shift housework as much as we

I Don't Want Peanuts!

could so we can focus on the things that mean more to us, like taking care of the children, traveling, and enjoying my husband. We both gladly pay the landscaper and my driver!

I don't apologize for the comforts I have because I need them. I work for them. I want the best. I don't apologize for it. You shouldn't either. If you are ready to keep going deeper and chasing your purpose, dreams, and where the money is at, come on. I got a whole lot mo' to tell you.

So if you want more than the peanuts, you have to go where the money is. In medical coding like in any industry, certain companies, departments, and services simply pay more. You want to go where you can get the big dollars. I am going to break this down for you shortly because yes you can make a lot of money in medical coding. I am not talking about medical billing.

I know the industry tends to market those two together. I don't dive down into insurance. I can't speak on the money expectation there, but over here for medical coding, we code the bill but do not deal in billing. So if someone tells you there is no money in medical billing, they may have a point. However, that is not my bread and butter; it's medical coding.

If you haven't gotten to the point where you need more, I will give you a few reasons for why you do. Do you have a 401k? Have you maxed out your savings plans, or 529? Do your children have vehicles? Have you paid off student loans and other debts? What about home ownership? Do you own your house or are you in a position to make passive income each month?

    I didn't have those things when I started in medical coding. I was rubbing pennies together. My cupboard wasn't filled with cobwebs but I wasn't eating steak and lobsters either. Peanut butter and jelly was more like it and anything quick. If you want to take care of your health, enjoy vacations, and see yourself on the other side of poverty, keep walking with me.

    My goal was to get bills paid for. One of my many reasons for why I got into medical coding, was to get out of debt and to travel. Then, I wanted more. So chase your dreams and believe in that while you are in school, working, studying, or getting mentoring from me or somebody to reach your goals. Don't stop dreaming but keep your mindset of extending your faith and desire to attain more.

    I have to tell you; some people are going to not like me for what I am about to say. If you want to make more, you will have to work more and not less. I know people sell programs and books about working less and getting something for nothing; don't waste your money. If you want to make money, you are going to have to work.

    The early bird catches the worm. So, sometimes, that means long nights, no showering, and doing whatever it takes to get it done. Those who said you would work less to make more–something is wrong. You'd better ask how that is possible because it is NOT!!

    If you want to make more you can. I know some

I Don't Want Peanuts!

people think they cannot do more, and they are tapped out. But if I said to reach your hand over your head and I will give you $50. Many people would do it in a heartbeat. Then, if I held $100 or $200 further in the air, people would nearly pop their back to stretch to get it if they really wanted it.

The question I ask new medical coders when they come to me about medical coding school is, do you really want it? You can enroll into any course and learn the material. You can take the courses and pass them with flying colors. However, if you want to make six figures in this industry, you will have to push yourself, especially in the beginning. Now, I didn't say it was over.

Just because you have to work hard doesn't mean you don't work smart. There are millions of ways to monetize your money and get more for your efforts. With more education and working the same job, you could get more. With more experience, you can also demand more. So finding the loopholes to make more while doing the same can work.

If anyone tells me they cannot make more–especially in medical coding, my response is that the person didn't want it bad enough to work for it. Some people are okay with complaining about their problems and doing nothing to solve them–I'm not. I am solution-driven, and whatever I set out to do, I must accomplish it.

I am that kind of mentor too! If you call me and ask how to get a job in medical coding, I ask, "What do you want?" What are you willing to work for? I can

Melvina W.

help you get the job, but I did NOT say it would be easy!

Once I get that answer, I know which fields to push them toward so they can build up to their goals. You can't always jump into the deep end if you can't swim and expect to survive. Some people who were thrown into the pool and couldn't swim failed, and their ambitions died. I don't want your dream to die. I want you to be coached on a process that can work with your education, experience, and goals.

I tell people in my podcast, named "Give Me Something To Work With!" If you are motivated, I can work with that. If you need to learn the course, no problem. If you finished school and need a job, I can work with it. If you need more directions within this field, I can work with it. Even if you need the certification guidance, I can work with it. But what I cannot do, is give you the desire to do this.

I Am Melvina Podcast

I can help you navigate how to make it when it comes to mindset for any field–and help people through mentorship. So, if you want the store, you have to prepare for the entry position and build up through management so you can learn the business. It is not so much about working your way up, but you have to pay your dues to learn the business so you can choose the best path for you.

Inpatient Diagnosis-Related Groups (DRGs) coders make more than Outpatient, Same Day Surgeries (SDS) coders get more than Outpatient coders. In other fields, you can work up and get six figures, but you will have to be indispensable. Building up your value is key. Some coders make 110K a year in my state of Georgia, while others can make 200K in places like Boston and San Francisco for coding. Different states pay more or less depending on their living expense factors for that area. Working in America, you can make great money in coding.

If you want to invest ten years in school to operate on the higher end, you can earn superb money. Keep in mind you are going to need housing, take care of your children, pay education tuition, etc. So, you need resources. You will need to pay people to help you make this money. Making more money means you will also spend more to keep managing the money. You will need to weigh the pros and cons.

The GOLDEN question is, can they work from home? Will they be more flexible for your family or families with children at home or taking care of older loved ones? At the same time, we have some professions that will not pay the same as medical coders but still require advanced college degrees, like educators/teachers. These are things to think about, hence the pros and cons. So, I am asking you, are you picking up what I am putting down?"

Think Box:

I told you all I have a podcast, "Give Me Something to Work With." I want to leave you with some food for thought. "My dear readers, listen to this...You can go to school to be a Medical Doctor (MD), Registered Nurse (RN), Lawyer, Engineer, and many other things and make very good money!

And please understand, I mean these professions working one job will pay more than a medical coder working one job. However, a medical coder with two jobs working from home doubling their income will give those people in those professions a run for their money. And medical coding takes about two or three months to learn and get employed with Infinity HIM School. How long does it take to become an MD, RN, Lawyer, Engineer, etc?

Why spend a fortune to learn an industry to make less than a medical coder, who could work two jobs, hit six figures, and do it from home?! What am I missing?

Other specialties in coding include Interventional Radiology, which will pay extremely well - I mean over 70k a year. And that is just for one coding job. What happens when you get another part-time job in the evenings for about 35k? Boom, there is the six FIGURES salary I am talking about.

But you cannot pop into these specialties of coding with very little training and education. You can start with Infinity HIM Medical Coding School to get the basics and enter this career for about $1,200. It is worth the investment based on the job market. We are a third of the cheaper medical coding schools – and we do this because this industry is a growing field with demand and job security if you are good.

My goal is to prepare medical coders to get and keep a job. Oftentimes, my students graduate and continue with me as their mentor to help them get the job. Now, if the students have a medical coding job, I help them keep the job. As they work it, I show them how to elevate on the job to reach their goals quicker.

When you work well, the company doesn't mind investing in you. Take these offers when they come. It will lead to more money in the end and help you to become indispensable. Always strive to increase your value in areas you can.

There are more fields of course you can look into, but I picked my niche based on the requirements to get in. Consider asking, how quickly can you learn and elevate in the department. How soon can you reach the next payment tier and the requirements for education.

My goal is to get you a job and fast-track you to get to six figures. If you are spending ten years in college, that means you are graduating with a ton of debt and pressure. (If you didn't finish, you really need to come to my school. You just wasted your money!) If you go to an affordable school, you can take entry jobs to build your experience and quickly surpass others because you want to have debt hovering over your head, adding stress.

If you choose to have one job you can make 50k to 60k a year with how I train my coders. If you want more than that, I can show you how to grow your income like I did. Another reason why I suggest not putting all your eggs in one basket, is because turnover happens. Getting fired is possible. So, knowing you have other options is a good thing to me.

To increase your options, you will need to learn more systems and increase your education to achieve higher-paying positions. But I believe knowing some tell-tale signs if you are getting fired might be good to share with you, too. If a company is thinking of "going in another direction," they will request a one-on-one conference with you. They will likely have a director, a team lead, and a slew of people present. If you have been making mistakes or your coding audits are not up to par weekly or monthly, the company could also have financial issues; they will request the "talk."

On the other side of the coin, in big meetings, you could be called in for something good. Usually, when you get a raise of more than $5 an hour, the management team seems to show up to congratulate you. So it doesn't have to be all bad. You want to pay attention to your work ethic, the feedback you get weekly, and whether you are meeting the job description and expectations of the company.

You don't always have as long as you need to learn a job. Sometimes, new coders think, oh, I am new, so it is acceptable. You may get passes for a week or

I Don't Want Peanuts!

While there are so many memories we've made over the years, one of the fondest is that of how we first met. As the old saying goes, she doesn't meet a stranger. While that is true of Melvina, what happens after is really up to the person she opens the opportunity to connect with. It is challenging to find people in whom there is a kindred type of connection and mindset. We chatted for quite a bit on the exhibit floor of that conference in Tennessee.

As I said to her that day, which has been a running joke between us all these years, "She was picking up what I was putting down!" The chat morphed into a group of us getting to know each other the rest of the conference through the meetings and meals each evening after the conference was over. It was the start of many, many, many memories over the years where, as both colleagues and friends, we would laugh hysterically and still build business and break bread together. That is a rare find for women like she and I who have such powerful energy.

Laquan Black

Melvina W.

Melvina is the epitome of resiliency, moving forward, making waves, and getting to the money no matter the obstacle. I appreciate seeing that in all she does, as it consistently serves to motivate me to push forward on my own path. Particularly, where business and finances are concerned.

This is precisely what she can teach others; how to tap into the mental fortitude to get at what you want no matter what it may be despite the obstacles that come....as she says often, "***Come HELL or High Water!***"

Regards,
Laquan Lauren Black, MSHIA, RHIA, CRIS, CAHIMS

two, but soon after, you are expected to perform. The medical field is not too flexible on mistakes. Too many of them will lead to you getting fired. So, if you are struggling on the job, call me before it gets serious if you need help! Again, I didn't say it was over…

Working online can be hard to pick up or read the signs you could notice a mile away if you were in person. If you are doing good, you will likely get compliments. Get asked management questions like, are you interested in growing with the company? They can bring up merit increases and other offers to show they are interested in you. If you are not getting those talks, it can also mean you are either in the middle of the pack or at the bottom.

When you have a job, it is the best time to go back to school especially if you are doing well. I am still getting certifications and learning new programs even now. If you hit a roadblock in getting a job, I would suggest looking at your resume and cover letter first. Something so simple as to how you present yourself at the onset could determine if a company will call youl back or not. You want to put your best foot forward and be matter-of-fact in your approach.

You want to highlight your core gifts like education, knowledge, experience, computer systems knowledge, degrees, and other related information. That will make a statement about you being you - and you being a good fit for the organization. I would like to learn more about your company and show you what I can do with your coding position.

Melvina W.

These are vague responses–to me. I like to chock my sentences full of meat so the people know exactly what to expect of me. You want to be assertive and not scared to negotiate your salary!

If you are stuck making 32k a year with experience, you need to call me. I am just going to put that straight. I can change the paradigm for you. I started with that amount (32k) when I got my first job, and that wasn't adequate back then. I remember when my base was 40k, and I could get overtime. I worked overtime as much as I could. I ended up making 75k that year. I loved making that money. So, in two to three years I started making that.

Now, stellar communication is a necessity when working online. You have to be good at establishing relationships through technology and that requires being a good communicator. Keep in mind, I am dealing with my hearing disability. I had to do the same job as others, and knew that my white counterparts were getting paid more for the same job. I saw people get hired after me, used me to do their job, and they received a promotion over me.

Don't allow these situations to discourage you. I would be lying or acting like the roses smell good and everything is all peaches and cream to say that if you are awesome, you will get everything you deserve. You might not. You will have to overcome something, like a resilient sponge.

I had to learn how to work with my disability and you will have to learn how to adapt to technology also. Stick to words you can clearly say. Check your emails before you send them to avoid the oops of pressing send prematurely. Work to be a professional so simple things don't become a problem.

I would tell you don't expect your managers to go above and beyond to help. If you don't know something, be resourceful. Google it, research it and try to figure it out if you can't get the support you need.

Some people are not rooting for you, true, but you have to make it ***"Come Hell or High Water"*** anyway. You have to be tactful and proactive, looking over the notes of doctors to help you code the diagnosis and procedures. Being detail-oriented will help you know how to code the diagnosis and procedures.

What I find, too, is most coding schools don't prepare you for a job. So it can be like getting cold water on your face when you get tired if you don't have a support system. I recommend my program because we show you how to code diagnoses and procedures.

I teach you how to code from the notes, procedures, and whatever else you get. I want to make sure you are prepared using real examples. Most schools teach no specialties, so you have a blanket understanding that is equivalent to whatever is presented in the book.

Take the time to pick the right school because it matters in getting a job. It breaks my heart to see people lose jobs from which I could have helped them save and build. I want you to know you are not alone; coding

Melvina W.

jobs can make you feel that way. Looking at a computer sitting by yourself can give you anxiety. You can lose your confidence, but if I am mentoring you, I can sit by you, or you can share your screen so I can help you get through your first day.

Read some of my reviews if you are struggling or haven't been able to get a job. I can help you find a specialty that can get you on the right track. If you want the store and not peanuts, having a second job is likely.

Never tell one company that you have another job. A company can get cold feet and think you are not committed. You may need to wake up early, I mean, like 5:00 am if you work two jobs. That's a long day of ten to twelve hours to pull off working two jobs. If you are not experienced, you might not want to do two jobs with overlapping schedules.

It can be extremely stressful doing that day in and day out. Stagger your jobs if you need or want to do two jobs to get more money. I recommend having a good morning routine to keep you motivated as you work on a computer. Smoothies, fruits and light food have kept my energy up better than candy and things like that. Drink water; please drink water if you want to take care of yourself.

It can be redundant work in this field. So, try to keep yourself energized and hydrated. If you have money goals, you will likely need two jobs to really pull off the money aspect, especially if you don't have the experience or education to pull a key position.

If progress is dragging on a job, it is okay to quit

a job for another one. However, make sure your mind is made up. Try to have a job or multiple job offers lined up to have a smooth transition. Don't settle for something less than you want. You can make it, and I assure you that you can.

If you are struggling with confidence, please get the ***Come Hell or High Water*** course and book. I know life can get hard, and making big money in this field is not easy. Nothing big is easy, but it can be simple. I can help you step out on faith.

My goal is to impact people's lives and show them they can do it. I help most people by providing them with a road map for getting into medical coding and making life make sense. If you need help to embrace your identity, check out Embrace Your Crown by Author K. Lee.

She is the guest host of Give Me Something to Work With," my podcast. She has published, I think, nearly 40 books and is working to get to 50. She is a wealth of information, support and a professional busi-

Melvina W.

ness owner. She is a great help to me running my CRM, business strategy and even publishing my books!

If you are stuck on what you should do, check out her series Embrace Your Crown, where she opens the gates to what has blocked your progress.

But once you know you want to go into medical coding, I can help you get the store and go way beyond the peanuts. I didn't say it was over. Turn the page to Chapter Seven. I am waiting.

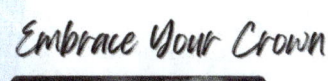

I Don't Want Peanuts!

Melvina W.

Transitioning to the Boss!

After you build experience and prove you can handle more, you can step into Management.

From 2005 to 2013, I worked jobs to build my career. It changed because of a life-altering experience, which was that I got three jobs. The twins were thirteen, and my oldest was sixteen. I had been married fifteen years at that point. People were always calling me for coders, and I couldn't take on any more jobs because I already had three! I had so many positions calling me, while I knew other coders without a job. I realized there was a gap between training them and being able to find and keep a job.

I knew it was a gift, mine—a business wrapped up as a present, and I was in the right position to take full advantage. To have something valuable to share with other people that they needed and I love to do, medical coding was a no-brainer to start my business. Medical coding was and still is my bread and butter. If I could show others how to do what I am doing, I felt that

Transitioning to the Boss!

was a win/win. I could help these companies find great coders and start a school to train better people who were certified.

I realized many people were trying to take the test after taking courses for years (spending tens of thousands of dollars) to finally get out and can't find a job. They didn't have what was necessary to get and keep any job. If you work in different disciplines, some things are more important than others. Many people miss out on employment opportunities because they have too much information or don't know how to apply what they have learned.

If you have never been to school, you are at the bottom, the beginning of your journey. I wanted to help people at the ground level because I could help the ambitious underdog to walk–into job prospects knowing how to compete with others in the field. I could help recently certified coders get a job if they couldn't before.

Going into an industry can be hard, no matter what you choose to do. In this field, you have to know something to prove yourself valuable or invaluable quickly, or they may move on. High turnover is everywhere, so you need to stand apart.

I help coders learn how to elevate their skills and zero in on getting a job in their discipline. Training others wasn't something I had thought about before. Although I helped my friends and people who asked me questions over the years, I was just trying to help; now, I see it as a business opportunity. This is what entrepreneurs do. They find problems and see how they can

Melvina W.

The Washington Family

As I have said numerous times, *time waits on no one*. This is my sentiments when I was faced with the unexpected death of my brother, Terry. I still miss him, especially when watching tv. Enjoy your family.

Transitioning to the Boss!
become part of the solution.

    I help coders learn the material they need in eight weeks to get a job! This was a huge problem for two groups, certified and uncertified coders. I got my degrees to work for me, and once more, I could share what I paid to learn with my students and mentees for a fraction of what other schools charge. What coding school can you take for under $1000 that will help you land a job?

    I am built differently, and I care about my students. I want you to win not just in medical coding but in life, too. So, a lot of what I do is offer education on how to learn medical coding and get your mindset right so you can apply my teachings to any career and in life. I wrote this book to share my journey so you know you can make it in medical coding, and with emphasis, I can help!

    This industry is ever-changing, and the money is great. I love this field, and I don't mind teaching it because I can make a difference with my process. You don't have to do everything I do, but you can dive into my mentoring to help you earn great money. This industry is steadily growing. I can tell you how to make great money and secure a job in this industry.

    Yes, there will be changes coming up ahead with AI, like in any industry. So, learning how to adjust to new technology and interacting with it is essential. You may get mad that AI is being used and not humans, but that won't change anything. Look at the advantage. Currently, AI is pulling out keywords from reports to help code. However, humans still need to review the code to confirm the work. The way you stay working is by learning how to use technology. Don't be afraid to learn what you don't know. This technology is in beta testing, so it will be more prevalent as the technology learns the field.

Over the years, I've understood what it is like to be a coder. Before I became a boss, manager, and mentor, I felt all the feelings you have. I asked the questions you wanted to ask–or need to ask. I am a wealth of information because I am not just here to teach you the book. I am here to show you how to present yourself for your desired job.

Becoming a boss has given me the chance to share my interview techniques, resume writing, and good follow-up emails to help you get a job! I have seen a lot of wrong ways to do this. Many times, what you are not saying is holding you back from a job. I am in an ideal position to break things down on another level for coders.

In my mentorship program, I am focused on the precise information I need to share with you. I am not here to teach just the textbook flow but to instruct on specific types of coding. I have had plenty of jobs, got hired and fired. I learned the dos and don'ts to help you navigate to win. I can shortcut your journey to earning more by mentoring you on what I know.

For my clients, I help prepare them for prospective jobs before they get them. I am here as long as you pay to keep me in your corner. I am not big on doing

Transitioning to the Boss!

things for free because people will dismiss it, and my time costs money. So I want to encourage you: Don't give away your stuff for free. Make people pay for it.

Believing in yourself is important in this field. You will be tested, but don't quit even if you think you might get fired. Call me so I can help you stay on that job. What doesn't kill you will make you stronger. I like to teach people how to enter this field so they may build upon their confidence. Your specialty and niche will be carved out as you get more acclimated to this industry. My focus is on entry-level positions, which are in high demand.

If you are struggling to get a job real quick, look at your resume. Look at your skills, computer skills and other knowledge related to coding. Don't overlook your experience. Be sure to have five references from the coding industry with letters behind their name. If you don't have five, start talking.

You have to go and meet people to get these references. They are very important to you getting a job or even receiving a phone call! You need to look at your references if you aren't getting the callbacks and only hearing crickets. You need to look at what you are missing. I have ten resumes at my disposal to submit for a job. You want to diversify your resume to submit the right one for the job.

Don't underestimate having a good personality. At the end of the day, the hiring director is a person, too. That person puts their pants on the same way you do. So, don't get intimidated. Know your worth and

Melvina W.

My fondest memory with Melvina is when she was here in Kenya. We had a great chitchat, and I shared my vision in life. She gave me a snippet of what it looks like to be Melvina (a go-getter and no-nonsense woman).

I have learned a lot from her. One of the most important things is hard work and being a go-getter. This has shaped a lot about how I approach my life. Her resilience and kindness have been a source of inspiration, and through her, I have gained a better understanding of how to stay motivated and nonchalant.

I am so grateful for so many things. Her kindness, encouragement, and guidance have truly impacted my life positively. She has enrolled me back in school; a dream I had only in my heart is now a reality.

Irene Mbithe

Transitioning to the Boss!

build your confidence. I talk about this because it really is essential.

If you are new to coding and that is making you second-guess stepping into this industry, don't stop. I love working with new coders who don't have any background or limited knowledge. New coders who ask questions will get far because there's a lot to learn in coding, and having someone like me who will be patient with you is necessary while you learn.

I work with experienced coders, but it can be a tug of war sometimes when they ask me questions they feel they have the answers to. Don't get me wrong; I am the biggest cheerleader of someone out here doing their thing no matter their industry. I will compliment you and then ask you how you are doing it. I want to learn, too.

But a piece of advice: if you are paying someone to help you, allow that person to help you. Why be on the phone with someone and ask them for help if you already know the answer?

The key is to stay quiet even if you know the answer; you just might learn something you didn't know before. As a learner student, move pride aside. Humble yourself to hear sound advice. Listening to others doesn't mean you are dumb. It makes you smart! Usually, the one who listens the most, knows the most.

When I went to school, it was popping for how many people enrolled. At the time of graduation, there were only a handful of us. Many people fail in this industry because they lose faith in themselves. Many people who invested 10k and 12k into a medical coding program cannot find a job because they were not prepared to get one. Schools are typically set up to train, not get you a job.

A lot of the people you see who you think are competing against you might not even be there. You need to get to a point where, even if they are, you are the right choice for the job. Who says you should only have one job to determine your salary and income? Stop putting limitations on yourself, and if you are going to work hard, have good reasons.

If you want to build your confidence to get a job, you can participate in the job training I offer to my mentorship clients. If you haven't seen medical coding implemented, it can be hard to learn. Having real case scenarios that you learn to code with me stepping you through it will ease your nerves.

I am still learning things. I don't know how those schools are still not preparing students to get jobs. I made my program inexpensive because I am working. I am making money. I do this to help people, and that's why I keep it affordable. My school is not as famous as others of note yet, but in time, it will be. The students who can pick up what I am putting down will be in a position to get a job.

For me, the metrics for how I judge my company is by the people who finish and get their desired job. Having a metric like that, you don't want to waste time on things that don't matter, like medical billing. My

Transitioning to the Boss!

Hermelyn LaTouche

My fondest memory of Melvina and me was meeting at one of our sorority conferences after we were free to walk the earth after the pandemic. It was like we were sisters because it was the first time we had spoken to each other in over a year. Little did we both know it would be the start of our journey together as friends, and now you can say that we are sisters. :)

I learned that I set my value not others and if others do not understand that then it is ok, there is a whole world of people and those who stick around understand my value.

I think she can teach others that your self-esteem is your self-esteem. You cannot let others tell you who you are, but you must know who you are. When you know who you are, you let that person walk into the room.

lane is coding. How insurance pays out is not relevant to medical coding. Most schools teach more about medical billing than medical coding. I am specific about what is going to get you in the door.

As a medical coding school owner, I have had the help of the KLE Business Concierge to organize my websites, CRM, and SEO. This is a business, and anything you want to get into will cost you money and time. You are going to need a team of some kind to help you. Don't get caught up in the small details. I pay people for that because I know it matters. Look at what you spend your time and money on, and if you don't get anything back, Houston, there is a problem!

Life is getting more expensive, and you must start to get things together to retire and take care of your family. I didn't say it was over because your children are grown. My daughters were teenagers when I started this business; I am still learning and growing.

There are better ways to do things; being open to making changes is how you can make it happen. Paying people will get you far. I don't cut my grass. I

Transitioning to the Boss!

don't cook. I code and teach others how to do the same. I have no shame in spending my time on what is paying me for what I like to do–medical coding and making more money.

Pitfall:

Don't be micromanaged; have top-notch Electronic Medical/Health Records (EMR/EHR) systems to work on (nothing outdated because it makes your life harder). Look at their expectations/product activity for the job. Some of the coding jobs are not worth it. If this is your first job, you might have to endure the challenges. But try to make it through and push yourself if they require it. If you are uncomfortable, look for a job daily if you feel you are at risk of getting fired. Don't get comfortable.

Learn to work smarter, not just harder. Medical coding has allowed me to work smart so that my hard work pays off. I have made back all the money I spent on education and my degrees, and some. How many people can tell you they are not in debt from school loans? That's another reason why I kept my school tuition low. I want you to stay out of debt so that you can invest in property and the stuff that matters.

Once more, my three pillars are money, family, and love. Each element is equally important because I need all of them to provide and care for the other. When you love people, you work. Your family needs your love and support. You cannot support people and take care of them without money.

So what do you want? What do you need? I didn't say it was over; I got a whole lot mo'!

Summary

Are you picking up what I am putting down?

By reading my first and second books, you should thoroughly understand the assignment. What did I say? Come Hell or High Water; we can, therefore we will…I Did Not Say It Is Over - we have a lot more to do through all of the challenges and be sure to "Let It Go."….the name of my next book, which is coming out by the Spring of 2025, "Let It Go." You want to get this collection if you need mental toughness to achieve your goals.

Life can be challenging but also rewarding. See you in the next book, and remember, if you are looking to shake things up, I am the medical coder you can trust. Because of my experiences, I am a wealth of information, and "I got a whole lotta mo to give."

"I didn't say it was over. Bye."

Melvina W.

Summary

Order Books!

Courses!

About the Author

Melvina W is a firm believer in Infinite Possibilities! She was born and raised in Savannah, Georgia, and more than exemplifies the true meaning of going above and beyond, believing the sky is the limit.

Melvina has more than 15 years of expertise in the Health Information Management (HIM) arena. She has worked for several hospitals across the United States, from Level One to Four, Teaching facilities, Trauma and Critical care units, and many more. She specializes in several medical coding disciplines.

Melvina also acquired a passion for coding and auditing charts for several Professional Service disciplines such as Inpatient, Observations, Consults, Clinics, and more. Melvina is infatuated with validating all coding assignments, modifiers, and diagnoses to ensure compliance with the HIM arena, and she loves solving "HIM problematic edits for Federal, State, and payer-specific regulations. Melvina has proven to be a person who collaborates with physicians to improve documentation to obtain the utmost reimbursement

About Melvina Washington

for the healthcare facility. In addition to coding, auditing, and compliance assignments, she is an excellent communicator, motivator, and team player who fully completes her projects and assignments with the highest confidentiality and accuracy possible.

In addition to her work, Melvina is the owner/founder and President of Infinity Health Information Management (HIM) and Infinity HIM School, where she has implemented an eight-week medical coding program for any potential persons who would like to break into the coding field. Melvina is changing the paradigm by teaching medical coding by focusing on a specific type of coding to create subject matter experts for faster turnaround of employment for the students.

Melvina has employed and assisted her students in gaining experience and advanced knowledge of the coding world. She offers training, education, resume assistance and interviewing techniques, consulting, and even job placement to qualified persons to gain real-world experience!

Melvina has a Master's in Business Administration with a concentration in Healthcare Management, a Bachelor's in Computer Information Systems, and an Associate's degree in Health Information Technology from the University of Phoenix. She is a Registered Health Information Technician (RHIT) with the American Health Information Management Association (AHIMA). She is also a Certified Professional Coder (CPC) with the American Academy of Professional Coders (AAPC). Melvina is a Georgia American Health Information Management Association (GAHIMA) and AAPC member. Attending meetings and networking

Melvina W.

with these organizations has enabled Melvina to correspond with other leaders in the industry and better coach her students.

Melvina has been a proud member of Zeta Phi Beta Sorority, Incorporated, since 2014 and has remained a member of Sigma Mu Zeta Chapter since her induction. She has been highly active within her chapter and volunteers in various community programs. Melvina believes in the power of giving back and placed 5th for all regions for March of Dimes under the Zeta Phi Beta Inc. individual fundraiser in 2019 and first place in 2020. She is a major contributor for the American Cancer Society, serves people experiencing homelessness, and plays bingo with seniors at nursing homes, among other activities.

In addition, Melvina owns the Infinite Beauty Blog and Black Cup of Joe platforms. Both blogs encourage women to chase their dreams and buy products and services to help make their lives and communities better. Melvina says, "I am blessed and fortunate," she feels she needs to share her story with other women looking for guidance to start or grow a business. She wrote and published her first book, Come Hell or High Water, and created a course for a deeper study.

About Melvina Washington

Melvina has been happily married to Glenn Feaster for 25 years and resides in Georgia. They are proud parents of three daughters who have graduated Historically Black Colleges/Universities. The oldest daughter, Mariama Aisha is working as a Meteorologist. She has her Masters and Bachelors degree and she is also a member of Zeta Phi Beta, Inc. The twins, Sierra Leone is working as a Special Education Teacher has her Bachelor's degree and attending school for her Masters degree and Amira Nkeiruka is working as a Civil En-

Melvina W. gineer has her bachelor's degree. Her three daughters are pursuing their dreams using the strong foundation Melvina and Glenn have implemented. Melvina's family is well-traveled. They have visited Canada, Mexico, France, Turkey, Italy, the United Kingdom, Egypt, Ghana, Togo, Australia, New Zealand, the Caribbean Islands, and over 30 States in the US so far.

Melvina's words to live by:

> "Do not be afraid of changing the paradigm. Make your own rules and follow them. Aggressively obtain financial education and wealth to leave a more secure, stabilized infrastructure for your family lineage. Believe that education creates options so you don't become complacent with your career or life. Expect the best; however, always have a backup plan and expect the unexpected. Remember always to give back, help others grow, and develop into what you have already come; pass it forward."

"Be yourself, dream big, work hard, play harder, and believe in infinite possibilities."

Melvina W., MBA, RHIT, CPC
Owner/President of Infinity HIM School, Infinite Beauty Possibilities, Black Cup of Joe Organizer, and Published Author/Mentor

Website: Infinityhim.com
Website: infinityhimschool.com
Website: jobinfinityhim.com
Website: IAmMelvina.com

About Melvina Washington
Website: IAMMelvinaW.com
Website: IAmMelvinaPodcast.com
Website: BlackCupofJoe.com
Website: InfiniteBeauty.blog

Email:
infinity@infinityhim.com or info@Iammelvina.com

SCAN ME

Call or Text:
770-240-0089 Press Extension 1
Web: KLEpub.com
Email Services@klepub.com

It's time to start and finish **YOUR Story!**

KLE Publishing specializes in helping people become authors. In as little as 15 to 90 days, we can help you develop your books and e-books and publish to 39,000 outlets! We also offer audiobook services.

Write, Edit, Format, Publish
We can help from
Start to Finish.

Explore and learn more about published authors affiliated with KLE.

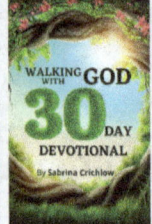

KLEPub.com

SCAN ME Or Use Link

Connect with KLE

Services to Launch or Grow Your Business for Authors & Product or Service based Companies

TURN
Key SOlution

Four Departments:

- Coaching and Consulting - Business SWOT Analysis
- Writing and Publishing Dept: Writing Services, Book/Ebook/Audio Book Services
- Business Concierge: Social Media, Web, CRM, and New Business Formulation Support: Message, Brand, Sales, Product Development, Strategy
- Production: Content Creation

www.ingramcontent.com/pod-product-compliance
Lightning Source LLC
Chambersburg PA
CBHW070110080526
44586CB00013B/1250